FROM THE BIBLE-TEACHING MINISTRY OF
CHARLES R. SWINDOLL

NAMES OF JESUS

There's just something about the name — *Jesus*. The name exalted above every other. The Word. The long-awaited King, spotless Lamb, and great I Am. Christ, Cornerstone, Shepherd, Servant . . . one title cannot begin to contain the vastness of the all-surpassing glory of Jesus.

If you've been looking for a concise resource that explains the significance of some of the Bible's most prominent names of Jesus, complete with real-world application, *Names of Jesus* will appeal to you.

Names of Jesus will empower you to:

- Discover the historical context of and prophecies fulfilled by the names of Jesus
- Answer confidently when asked about Jesus
- Be inspired to worship Jesus as you gain a richer understanding of who He is

There's only one name under heaven with the power to save, and that name is Jesus. Get to know the name.

CHAPTER : VERSE

NAMES OF JESUS

From the Bible-Teaching Ministry of Charles R. Swindoll

Charles R. Swindoll has devoted his life to the accurate, practical teaching and application of God's Word and His grace. A pastor at heart, Chuck has served as senior pastor to congregations in Texas, Massachusetts, and California. Since 1998, he has served as the founder and senior pastor-teacher of Stonebriar Community Church in Frisco, Texas, but Chuck's listening audience extends far beyond a local church body. As a leading program in Christian broadcasting since 1979, *Insight for Living* airs in major Christian radio markets around the world, reaching people groups in languages they can understand. Chuck's extensive writing ministry has also served the body of Christ worldwide and his leadership as president and now chancellor of Dallas Theological Seminary has helped prepare and equip a new generation of men and women for ministry. Chuck and Cynthia, his partner in life and ministry, have four grown children, ten grandchildren, and four great-grandchildren.

Published By
IFL Publishing House, A Division of Insight for Living Ministries
Post Office Box 1050, Frisco, Texas 75034-0018

Editor in Chief: Cynthia Swindoll, President, Insight for Living Ministries
Executive Vice President: Wayne Stiles, Th.M., D.Min., Dallas Theological Seminary
Writers: Derrick Jeter, Th.M., Dallas Theological Seminary
Kelley Mathews, Th.M., Dallas Theological Seminary
Lisa Robinson, Th.M., Dallas Theological Seminary
Sharifa Stevens, Th.M., Dallas Theological Seminary
Substantive Editors: Jim Craft, M.A., English, Mississippi College; Certificate of Biblical and Theological Studies, Dallas Theological Seminary
Kathryn Robertson, M.A., English, Hardin-Simmons University
Copy Editor: Paula McCoy, B.A., English, Texas A&M University-Commerce
Project Supervisor, Creative Ministries: Megan Meckstroth, B.S., Advertising, University of Florida
Project Coordinator, Publishing: Melissa Cleghorn, B.A., University of North Texas
Proofreader: LeeAnna Swartz, B.A., Communications, Moody Bible Institute
Designers: Mark Burgdorff, B.A., Photojournalism Communications, Stephen F. Austin State University
Margaret Gulliford, B.A., Graphic Design, Taylor University
Production Artist: Nancy Gustine, B.F.A., Advertising Art, University of North Texas

ISBN: 978-1-62655-053-7
Printed in the United States of America

TABLE OF CONTENTS

CHAPTER:VERSE

A LETTER FROM CHUCK

He was like no one else.

Jesus was a popular teacher. He explained Scripture as no one else could do. He healed the sick. He forgave people's sins. He even raised the dead. Soon the question began sweeping the country: "Who is this man?"

How many times did people utter those words while Jesus walked the earth?

Who is this man? the disciples gasped after witnessing Jesus subdue a great storm with just a word.

Who is this man? the Pharisees whispered when Jesus forgave a woman of ill repute.

Who is this man? Herod Antipas asked after hearing about the healings and teachings of Jesus, even after murdering His cousin, John the Baptist.

You remember that classic scene in *Romeo and Juliet* when Juliet ponders aloud the nature of names? She is in love with Romeo, a son of the Montague family — rivals of her family, the Capulets. *"O, be some other name!"* she pleads. She goes on:

> *What's in a name? that which we call a rose*
> *By any other name would smell as sweet.*[1]

Of course, things don't exactly end well for Romeo and Juliet. It turns out, in their world, names do matter, and not even their love can conquer all.

Names matter in our world, too — certainly one name more than any other.

Jesus.

Because of the sacrifice of Jesus, the Son of God, you and I can be called God's daughters and sons. Jesus isn't some cold, compassionless stranger. The Son of Man knows us from experience. He understands our struggles, having been tempted in every way but remaining without sin (Hebrews 4:15). The Son of God redeemed us from death. Jesus' love conquers all. Just as in many cultures brides take on the names of their grooms, believers in Christ take on His name and share in His inheritance forever.

What's in His name? *Everything.* He is fully God and fully man. That's why His is "the name above all other names" (Philippians 2:9 NLT).

Two millennia have passed since Jesus walked this earth, and yet people are still baffled about who He is. Is He God? Man? A good teacher? The Messiah? All of the above — or none?

In the public square, you'll hear all kinds of opinions about Jesus. Ideas about His birth, ministry, death, and resurrection. It's been that way down through the centuries. That's why Jesus asked the disciples a question that echoes to today: *"Who do you say that I am?"*

Your answer to that question matters more than anything else in this life.

Whether you've never met Him or you've known Him for decades, if you're curious about how Jesus is described in both the Old and New Testaments, the book you hold in your hands is for you. This compact yet in-depth resource will shine a new light on the Savior, inform your worship, and strengthen your trust as you investigate the many names of Jesus. From the preincarnate appearances of the Angel of the Lord in the Old Testament . . . to the Alpha and Omega in the book of Revelation. Within these pages, you'll discover how each name contributes to our understanding of who Jesus is and why His names matter.

"But who do you say that I am?" Jesus asked. Peter promptly responded, "You are the Messiah sent from God!" (Luke 9:20). My hope is that after reading this book, you, too, will be able to answer with the same zeal and confidence when *you* are asked who Jesus is.

In the hope of His marvelous name,

Charles R. Swindoll

---

1. William Shakespeare, *Romeo and Juliet*, Arden Shakespeare, 2nd ed., ed. Brian Gibbons, 1980, 2.2.42–44, http://shakespeare.mit.edu/romeo_juliet/full.html (accessed July 8, 2014).

NAMES
OF JESUS

CHAPTER : VERSE

ANGEL OF THE LORD

f all the mysteries in the Old Testament, one of the most fascinating is the identity of *malak Yahweh* — the Angel of the Lord. Whenever He made an appearance, He was never treated as a mere angel but as divine. When the Angel of the Lord appeared to Hagar in the wilderness to comfort her with a promise, she recognized that God was speaking to her (Genesis 16:7–13). The same was true for Abraham, Jacob, Moses, Joshua, and Gideon.

However, none of them realized (or could have understood) that the Angel of the Lord was the preincarnate Christ — the human-like manifestation of Jesus *before* He became human. Only by looking back through the New Testament can we see the similarities between Jesus and the Angel of the Lord.

Specifically, those similarities are evident in the realms of revelation, commissioning, protection, intercession, advocacy, comfort, and judgment.

Revelation

While in the burning bush, the Angel of the Lord disclosed God's covenant-making name: I Am (Exodus 3:2, 4, 6, 14). In the New Testament, Christ also revealed God's name (John 17:6) — by word and by deed, claiming the name of God for Himself (8:58).

Commissioning

The Angel of the Lord called Moses to deliver Israel from Egypt (Exodus 3:7–8), Gideon to deliver Israel from the Midianites (Judges 6:11–23), and Samson (through his parents) to deliver Israel from the Philistines (13:1–21). Likewise, Christ called and commissioned His disciples to preach the message of deliverance from sin to men and women in every nation (Matthew 28:19–20; John 20:21).

Deliverance

The Angel of the Lord was Israel's source of salvation from the Egyptians, the Midianites, and the Philistines. Christ delivers believers from the fear, guilt, and penalty of sin (Ephesians 1:7; Hebrews 2:14–15), and in the future, He will deliver Israel once and for all (Romans 11:25–26).

Protection

The Angel of the Lord sheltered Israel in David's day (Psalm 34:7) and safeguarded King Hezekiah from the Assyrian army (2 Kings 19:35). Similarly, Christ protects believers from fear (Hebrews 13:5–6).

Intercession

The Angel of the Lord prayed for Jerusalem (Zechariah 1:12–13). And Christ, our High Priest, intercedes for us (Hebrews 7:25).

Advocacy

The Angel of the Lord was the champion for sinful believers

against the accusations of Satan (Zechariah 3:1–7). Christ, likewise, is our righteous Advocate, defending our righteousness gained by His work on the cross (1 John 2:1–2).

Comfort

The Angel of the Lord found the outcast and despondent Hagar and promised her safety and a future (Genesis 16:7–13). Christ ministered to the outcast (John 9:35–38; 16:1–4) and blessed the brokenhearted (Isaiah 61:1; Luke 4:16–19).

Judgment

The Angel of the Lord punished Israel for David's census (1 Chronicles 21:14–17) and commanded David to build an altar (21:18). Christ, during the great tribulation, will judge His people Israel along with unbelievers living on the earth (Matthew 25:31–41; 2 Thessalonians 1:5–10). Once the earth is purged, the temple will be rebuilt for worship (Ezekiel 43:2–5, 12).

Once Christ was born, the Angel of the Lord ceased to appear because He now took on human flesh, proving that who Christ was and what He did as the Angel of the Lord matched who He was and what He did as

The Angel of the Lord found the outcast and despondent Hagar and promised her safety and a future.

the incarnate Son of God. And who Christ was and what He did in the past matches who Christ is and what He does in the present (Hebrews 13:8). If we need deliverance, Christ can deliver us. If we need revelation, Christ can guide us. If we need forgiveness, Christ can advocate for us. If we need comfort, Christ can comfort us. If we need prayer, Christ can intercede for us.

— *Derrick G. Jeter*

SHILOH

"The scepter shall

not depart from Judah,

Nor the ruler's staff from

between his feet,

Until Shiloh comes,

And to him shall be the

obedience of the peoples."

— Genesis 49:10

f all the names of Jesus, Shiloh may be the least known. Shiloh is mentioned only *once* in the Bible in reference to a person — in Genesis 49:10. The verse has been the subject of vibrant discussion among academics, who ask, *What is this word? To whom does it refer?*

Some scholars transliterate (or write phonetically) the word *Shiloh* and regard it as a proper noun. In this case, "Shiloh . . . is a name for the coming Messiah." [1] The NASB and KJV translations of the Bible both do this.

Other scholars translate *Shiloh,* citing long-standing translations of Hebrew Scripture — the Septuagint and Targums — to back their decision. [2] Thus, their reading of Genesis 49:10 is: "Nor the ruler's staff from between his feet, *until he* comes *to whom it belongs;* the nations will obey him" (NET, emphasis added).

Whether they translate or transliterate *Shiloh,* experts are unified that the word describes a person. They also agree that Genesis 49:10 is prophetic, referring specifically to the Davidic dynasty (from the tribe of Judah) and, ultimately, the Messiah. [3] First-century Jewish manuscripts validate their view.

Outside of Genesis 49, *Shiloh* generally refers to a place. Joshua built the tabernacle at Shiloh as the people of Israel finally inherited the Promised Land (Joshua 18:1). In the wilderness, Moses had originally constructed the tabernacle as the place where men could meet with God through prayer, offer sacrifices, and receive atonement for sin. The physical presence of God was *visible* during the tabernacle days (Exodus 40:34–38). God, appearing as a pillar of cloud or fire, led the Israelites into rest (Joshua 22:4).

In the same way, Jesus leads us into rest in both the present and the future. About the future, He said, "I go to prepare

God has always desired

to be present in the lives of His

people — including our lives,

right now.

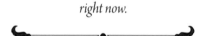

a place for you. If I go and prepare a place for you, I will come again and receive you to Myself, that where I am, there you may be also" (John 14:2–3).

Today, we don't have divine pillars of cloud and fire, but we have guidance just like the people of Israel who camped around Shiloh had, because the Spirit of God dwells with us, helping us to abide in Jesus (14:25–26; 15:4).

In Genesis, God walked in the garden in the cool of the day (Genesis 2:8). He talked to Moses face-to-face, like friends do

(Exodus 33:11). Jesus expressed how earnestly He desired to spend Passover with the disciples just hours before His crucifixion (Luke 22:14–15). God has *always* desired to be present in the lives of His people — including our lives, right now. The love of Jesus is a relentless pursuit to make God's kingdom a dwelling place with His people, forever.

> "Behold, the tabernacle of God is among men, and He will dwell among them, and they shall be His people, and God Himself will be among them, and He will wipe away every tear from their eyes; and there will no longer be any death; there will no longer be any mourning, or crying, or pain; the first things have passed away." And He who sits on the throne said, "Behold, I am making all things new." (Revelation 21:3–5)

— *Sharifa Stevens*

1. *Nelson's New Illustrated Bible Commentary: Spreading the Light of God's Word into Your Life*, gen. ed. Earl D. Radmacher (Nashville: Thomas Nelson, 1999), 81.
2. Victor P. Hamilton, "Shiloh," in *Theological Wordbook of the Old Testament*, vol. 2, gen. ed. R. Laird Harris (Chicago: Moody Press, 1980), 919.
3. H. G. Andersen, "Shiloh," in *The Zondervan Pictorial Encyclopedia of the Bible*, gen. ed. Merrill C. Tenney (Grand Rapids: Zondervan, 1976), 404.

I AM

ften during His ministry, Jesus avoided directly answering the question so many wondered: *Are you the Messiah?* But during one verbal sparring match with the Jewish religious leaders, Jesus didn't wait to be asked. He told them, "Your father Abraham rejoiced to see My day, and he saw it and was glad" (John 8:56).

They scoffed at Him, "You are not yet fifty years old, and have You seen Abraham?" (8:57).

Jesus replied with the defining statement: "Truly, truly, I say to you, before Abraham was born, I am" (8:58).

Jesus wasn't mixing up His present and past tenses. No, He knew exactly what

He was saying, and so did the Pharisees. He was claiming to be God. Specifically, He was equating Himself with Yahweh — the God of Abraham, Isaac, and Jacob . . . the Jews' covenant God whom they worshiped at the temple. No wonder the Pharisees picked up stones!

The name I Am goes back to the beginning of Moses' ministry when he met God at the burning bush in the wilderness. There before the flames, Moses wanted reassurance that his Hebrew brothers would accept his word about their God:

> Then Moses said to God, "Behold, I am going to the sons of Israel, and I will say to them, 'The God of your fathers has sent me to you.' Now they may say to me, 'What is His name?' What shall I say to them?" God said to Moses, "I Am Who I Am"; and He said, "Thus you shall say to

the sons of Israel, 'I Am has sent me to you.'" (Exodus 3:13–14)

The Hebrew word for "I Am" is *hayah* — a form of the verb "to be." *Hayah* denotes God's timelessness, His everlasting existence,

Like the Samaritan woman

and the Pharisees, we have

the opportunity to respond to

Jesus, the I Am.

and His self-existence. Some English translations use the future tense, "I will be who I will be." Also known to Jews simply as "the name," *Hayah* was so respected that it was not spoken aloud. Instead, the Jews substituted other letters and added vowels, giving us the name *Jehovah* or *Yahweh*. In our English Bibles, this name is written as Lord. Yahweh is God's personal name, the only one that He gave Himself:

God, furthermore, said to Moses, "Thus you shall say to the sons of Israel, 'The LORD [Yahweh], the God of your fathers, the God of Abraham, the God of Isaac, and the God of Jacob, has sent me to you.' This is My name forever, and this is My memorial-name to all generations." (Exodus 3:15)

Jesus invoked the I Am name another time — during His encounter with the Samaritan woman at the well:

> The woman said to Him, "I know that Messiah is coming (He who is called Christ); when that One comes, He will declare all things to us." Jesus said to her, "I who speak to you am He." (John 4:25–26)

This recognizable claim to deity evoked a completely different reaction from the woman than it did from the Pharisees. She responded with belief and action, leaving her waterpot behind to tell all she encountered to come and meet the Christ (4:28–29).

Like the Samaritan woman and the Pharisees, we have the opportunity to respond to Jesus, the I Am. The woman was amazed and ran to tell her townspeople of this man who knew all about her. The Pharisees picked up stones to kill Him. May *we* respond with belief, and may we rest in the knowledge that Jesus Christ is not merely a great prophet or miracle-worker. He is God Himself, the Son, the second person of the Trinity — the everlasting I Am.

— *Kelley Mathews*

WONDERFUL COUNSELOR

For a child will be

born to us, a son

will be given to us;

And the government

will rest on

His shoulders;

And His name

will be called

Wonderful

Counselor.

— Isaiah 9:6

From time to time, we all need wise counsel. In legal disputes, it's foolish not to have a lawyer. When making important financial decisions, it's prudent to talk to an advisor. And students are keen to seek guidance when going off to college or beginning their careers. It's a complex world, and the wise know we can't successfully navigate it alone.

But human counselors, while often helpful, are fallible. Only one is utterly reliable, perpetually available, and absolutely affordable — Jesus.

Before the birth of Jesus, God provided counsel through His prophets. All too often, however, those in power refused to listen. Such was the case with the foolish King

Ahaz, who forced the nation of Judah to suffer by refusing to listen to the prophet Isaiah. With war looming on the horizon, the

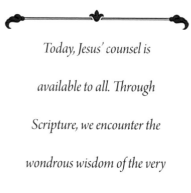

Today, Jesus' counsel is

available to all. Through

Scripture, we encounter the

wondrous wisdom of the very

mind of God.

Lord promised to anoint another king — one who would need no teachers, mentors, or advisors to guide Him because He Himself would bear the name "Wonderful Counselor" (Isaiah 9:6).

In Hebrew, the name reads *pehleh yawats,* which literally translates: "Wonder of a Counselor," meaning that Jesus' words — His teaching — would be exceptional and distinguished from mere human counsel. Both the Old and the New Testaments

attest that Jesus, indeed, lived up to such expectations.

The first part of the book of Isaiah derides human wisdom as folly and lacking in spiritual wisdom (5:20–21). In contrast, Jesus, as highlighted in the Messianic passage of Isaiah 9:6, gives wondrous wisdom. The Spirit of the Lord rests on Him, giving Him wisdom that transcends human understanding and insight (11:2). Such divine wisdom — such wonderful counsel — includes the perplexing truth that weakness is strength, surrender is victory, and death is life (53:1–12). As the Wonderful Counselor, Jesus carried that wisdom into the New Testament when He taught that a grain of wheat must die in order to bear fruit and that the one who wants life must deny life (John 12:24–26).

More than two millennia later, Jesus' counsel is still sought by sages and simpletons, princes and paupers, leaders and laborers, kings and capitalists, spiritualists and secularists. As it did when He was ministering on earth, Jesus' wisdom continues to astonish and awe. By any measure, His teaching bears the marks not just of greatness but of wonder and magnificence. No other individual has possessed such divine wisdom and has changed so many lives because of His teaching. So whatever we might think of Solomon, Buddha, Confucius, Plato, Aristotle, or other wise individuals, Jesus stands first.

Today, Jesus' counsel is available to all. Through Scripture, we encounter the wondrous wisdom of the very mind of God. Along with the psalmist we, too, can confess:

> Your testimonies
> [God] . . . are my
> delight;
> They are my counsel-
> ors. (Psalm 119:24)

And if we reject the ways of Ahaz and listen and learn from the counsel of the Word, we'll discover we are blessed (119:2).

However, in order to fully understand the wisdom of the Wonderful Counselor, we must first surrender our minds and spirits *to* the wondrous Counselor — we must come to faith in Jesus Christ and receive the gift of the Holy Spirit. If you've not done so, or if you're unsure, please read "How to Begin a Relationship with God" at the back of this book. Once you've given yourself to Christ, He promises to send you the Holy Spirit who will "guide you into all truth," including the exceptional wisdom of Jesus — our Wonderful Counselor.

— Derrick G. Jeter

PRINCE OF PEACE

For a child will be

born to us, a son will

be given to us;

And the government

will rest on His shoulders;

And His name

will be called

Wonderful Counselor,

Mighty God,

Eternal Father,

Prince of Peace.

— Isaiah 9:6

In a world consumed with strife, conflict, and war, nothing is more divine than peace. That's why Jesus called peacemakers "sons of God" (Matthew 5:9). To those who live in the safe enclaves of suburbia among the "civilized" class, *peace* is just another word. But to those who live in nations ravaged by war or on the crime-infested streets of the inner city or behind whitewashed doors hiding abusive households, *peace* isn't just another word — it's a divine word.

Nothing calms the savage soul like *shalom* — the peace of God. But God's peace rarely comes through what we might consider "normal" means like diplomats and peacekeepers. Rather, it usually comes through "abnormal" means, and the ultimate source of peace came as a surprise to all who heard of it.

During a time when war hung heavy in the air, when King Ahaz's sinful stubbornness brought the nation of Judah to near ruin, the Lord promised to anoint another king — a faithful king who would be born in due time (Galatians 4:4) and whose future, one-thousand-year reign would be marked by peace. The

In His death, therefore, Jesus accomplished what made Him Prince of Peace. And in His resurrection, He was crowned Prince of Life.

prophet Isaiah wrote of this coming king: "For a child will be born to us, a son will be given to us" (Isaiah 9:6).

In the original Hebrew, *child* is in the emphatic position, meaning this child would not only be God come to earth, but God born on earth — "a son" to represent His humanity, "given

to us" to represent His divinity. This child would possess traits that demonstrated God's presence on earth — His divine and human kingship, His Immanuel sign (7:14) — described in four compound titles: "Wonderful Counselor, Mighty God, Everlasting Father, Prince of Peace" (9:6 NLT).

The climax of this royal child's rule would be peace — a peace that will forever produce serenity and security (32:17). The child, of course, was none other than Jesus Christ. Christ's peace is *pacis omnimodae* — a covenant of peace of every kind (Ezekiel 34:25): outward and inward, of country and conscience, temporal and eternal. And though He came from the line of Judah — the lion of Israel (Genesis 49:9; Matthew 2:6) — the Christ child came in peace as Prince (Acts 5:31), born of the "God of peace" (Romans 16:20) and announced from heaven with a song of peace (Luke 2:14).

Jesus establishes peace, not by brutally squashing defiance to His rule, but by practicing submission and meekness to make defiance pointless, so that through His death, we as sinful people might be reconciled to a holy God. In His death, therefore, Jesus accomplished what made Him Prince of Peace. And in His resurrection, He was crowned Prince of Life (Acts 3:15).

At the close of His earthly ministry, Jesus bid farewell with a message of peace (John 14:27), leaving to us the ministry of peace (2 Corinthians 5:18–19), so that we, and all who follow the Prince of Peace, might be children of peace.

God's answer to everything that terrorizes us — from bullies to abusers, despots to tyrants, conflicts to wars — is *the* Child, the Prince of Peace. And as the Prince of Peace, Jesus promises to give us His peace (John 14:27). If we would but rest in that promise, the things that terrorize us would mysteriously lose their power, and we would find ourselves calm of heart and head — no longer afraid, for the Child of Peace has entered in.

— *Derrick G. Jeter*

BRANCH

Then a shoot will

spring from the

stem of Jesse,

And a branch

from his roots

will bear fruit.

— Isaiah 11:1

The Bible often uses metaphors to explain profound ideas by linking lofty truths to earthly objects. One poetic example is the tree. We're accustomed to describing our ancestry as a "family tree." In a similar way, the prophets spoke of Jesus metaphorically, describing Him as "a righteous Branch," the One who would flourish eternally.

Jeremiah 23:5 reads:

"Behold, the days are coming,"
  declares the LORD,
"When I will raise up for David a
  righteous Branch;
And He will reign as king and act
  wisely
And do justice and righteousness
  in the land."

In Jesus' family tree, the root is Jesse, David's father (Isaiah 11:1). David, along with his kingdom of Israel, is the trunk. King David was a man after God's own heart, and God covenanted with David, saying,

> "When your days are complete and you lie down with your fathers, I will raise up your descendant after you, who will come forth from you, and I will establish his kingdom. He shall build a house for My name, and I will establish the throne of his kingdom forever." (2 Samuel 7:12–13)

After David's son Solomon's reign and as a result of Israel's infidelity to God, the kingdom of Israel was severed — like a flourishing tree chopped down to a lowly stump.

No hope of life seemed possible for that hacked up family tree . . . but God is able to cause life to spring forth from death.

His plan was to raise up a descendant who would come forth from David's line to rule over not only an earthly kingdom but an eternal kingdom.

This descendant, Jesus, was often called "the Nazarene" (Mark 16:6; Luke 24:19; John 19:19; Acts 22:8) because He grew up in Nazareth (Matthew 21:11). Nazareth, located in a fertile valley, was

People of Jesus' day

literally referred

to Him as the

Branch Man!

known for its mild climate and flourishing flowers and fruit.[1] That which could not grow in other regions could sprout and thrive here.

The root word of both "Nazarene" and "Nazareth" is *netser* . . . also translated as "branch."[2] How poetic! The reference to the Branch would not be lost on devout Jews who spoke Aramaic or Hebrew and who were familiar with messianic prophecy.

That's why Matthew wrote in his gospel: "This was to fulfill what was spoken through the prophets: 'He shall be called a Nazarene'" (Matthew 2:23). People of Jesus' day literally referred to Him as the Branch Man! Subsequently, Jesus' followers were sometimes referred to as the Nazarenes. And that name continues. Even now, there are regions in the Middle East where persecuted brothers and sisters are labeled *Nasrani* — Arabic for "Nazarenes."

Because of the saving power of Jesus Christ, the Nazarene, the Branch, we have an ever-flourishing hope — in place of death and sin's relentless hacking at our lives. We who believe have been grafted into this regal family tree (Romans 11:17–24). We bear the fruit of righteousness when we abide in Him (John 15:5). We, too, are Branch men and women.

— *Sharifa Stevens*

1. J. W. Charley, "Nazareth," in *New Bible Dictionary*, 2nd ed., ed. J. D. Douglas and others (Downers Grove, Ill.: InterVarsity, 1991), 819.
2. A. F. Walls, "Nazarene," in *New Bible Dictionary*, 2nd ed., ed. J. D. Douglas and others (Downers Grove, Ill.: InterVarsity, 1991), 818–19.

JESUS

Perhaps the most widely known name in human history, at least since AD 30, Jesus is the Greek variation of the Hebrew name Joshua or Yeshua. Both names mean "the LORD (Yahweh) saves." Just as Joshua, son of Nun, was Yahweh's tool to bring the chosen people victoriously into the Promised Land, Jesus also leads His chosen people — those who believe in Him — into His heavenly kingdom. His name has both purpose and power.

We first get a glimpse of the purpose of Jesus' name when the angel who appeared to Joseph in a dream told him, "You shall call His name Jesus, for He will save His people from their sins" (Matthew 1:21). Months later, on the night Jesus was born, a heavenly host appeared to shepherds in nearby fields, proclaiming that a Savior had been born to them (Luke 2:11). Eight days later, Mary and Joseph presented the baby in the temple for dedication, naming Him Jesus, "the name given by the angel before He was conceived in the womb" (2:21). The two gospel accounts complement each other to give a fuller picture of Jesus' coming.

Perhaps the original readers, more familiar with the etymology of Jesus' name, would have connected it to His purpose each time the text referred to Jesus by name. Modern-day readers do not have that connection to the original language, but we do have the New Testament, in which its writers remind us that in Jesus alone we find salvation.

> But when the kindness of God our Savior and His love for mankind appeared, He saved us, not on the basis of deeds which we have done in righteousness, but according to His mercy, by the washing of

> regeneration and renewing by the Holy Spirit, whom He poured out upon us richly through Jesus Christ our Savior. (Titus 3:4–6)

In addition to revealing His purpose for coming, the name of Jesus holds power. After His death and resurrection, Jesus' followers performed miracles in His name. In Acts 3, Peter healed a lame beggar, then addressed the crowd that

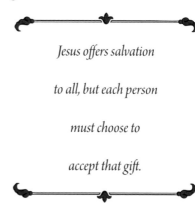

Jesus offers salvation

to all, but each person

must choose to

accept that gift.

had gathered in amazement: "On the basis of faith in His name, it is the name of Jesus which has strengthened this man whom you see and know" (Acts 3:16). But these healings were not performed using a sort of magical incantation, as meddlers in the occult might attempt to do. Rather, the person healing someone "in the name of Jesus" acted as His representative, filled with His power because His Spirit lived within.

Beyond physical healing, though, everyone can experience the power inherent in Jesus' name by trusting in Him alone for salvation from the power of sin and death. Such deliverance can only be found in Him: "There is salvation in no one else; for there is no other name under heaven that has been given among men by which we must be saved" (Acts 4:12).

Jesus offers salvation to all, but each person must choose to accept that gift (Ephesians 2:9). At the end of time, when Jesus returns as triumphant King, the words of Paul in Philippians 2 will be fulfilled: "At the name of Jesus every knee will bow, of those who are in heaven and on earth and under the earth, and that every tongue will confess that Jesus Christ is Lord, to the glory of God the Father" (Philippians 2:10–11).

How will we kneel — as conquered enemies or humble, grateful believers in Yeshua, Jesus, the Savior?

— *Kelley Mathews*

IMMANUEL

While most expectant parents must decide what they will name their baby, Mary and Joseph were spared that particular task. When the angel appeared to Joseph in a dream to assure him that Mary's child was indeed divine, he told Joseph what name they were to give the child. Here we read the familiar words, "She will bear a Son; and you shall call His name Jesus, for He will save His people from their sins" (Matthew 1:21). Joseph was to take Mary as his wife knowing that her child truly was the Son of God.

But then Matthew added his commentary on the angel's statement: "Now all this took place to fulfill what was spoken by the Lord through the prophet [Isaiah]: 'Behold, the virgin shall be with child and shall bear a Son, and they shall call His name Immanuel,' which translated means, 'God with us'" (Matthew 1:22–23).

How did Jesus as Immanuel fulfill a prophecy from Isaiah? Let's explore the original context first.

Isaiah the prophet was confronting Ahaz, the ungodly king of Judah, who was considering a treaty with Assyria in order to fend off an attack from Syria and Israel from the north. Isaiah warned Ahaz not to make that treaty, assuring him that the Lord would save Judah another way. Though urged by Isaiah to ask the Lord for a sign that this would truly happen, Ahaz refused. Isaiah replied:

> "Therefore the Lord Himself will give you a sign: Behold, a virgin will be with child and bear a son, and she will call His name Immanuel." (Isaiah 7:14)

The Hebrew word used here for "virgin" is *almah*, meaning maiden, "a young woman,"

which can apply to any unmarried woman of childbearing age or to a married woman who has not yet given birth to a child.[1] Scholars differ on the identity of the child born during Ahaz's time to fulfill Isaiah's prophecy regarding the kings of Israel and Syria. But all agree that God was reassuring Ahaz of His close presence during the political situation facing Judah. The child would be a sign to Ahaz — when Judah was spared, as God had foretold — that God was with His people.

When Matthew, more than seven hundred years later, cited Isaiah's words in reference to Jesus' birth, the gospel writer declared Jesus as the Messiah, God's ultimate fulfillment of the prophecy. He chose to translate *almah* with a similar term, yet one that contained a narrower meaning. The Greek term he used, *parthenos*, can only mean a chaste young woman who has never had sexual relations.[2] In this way, Matthew emphasized Mary's physical virginity (Matthew 1:25) and highlighted the miraculous circumstances of Jesus' conception and birth. This child would not be a typical baby but the Son of God, God Himself in human form. In coming to His people in such a way, Jesus embodied the con-

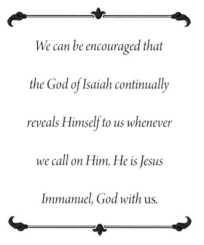

We can be encouraged that

the God of Isaiah continually

reveals Himself to us whenever

we call on Him. He is Jesus

Immanuel, God with us.

cept of "God with us," whereas the child of Ahaz's time merely symbolized God's presence. Jesus *became* Immanuel. He entered time and space to join His chosen people as part of His grand redemption scheme. This declaration would have resonated with and comforted Matthew's original, mostly Jewish, readers.

Jesus remains Immanuel even today. At His Ascension, He told His followers, "And lo, I am with you always, even to the end of the age" (Matthew 28:20). Through His Spirit sent to His disciples at Pentecost and bestowed on every believer since, Jesus abides with us intimately. We can be encouraged that the God of Isaiah continually reveals Himself to us whenever we call on Him. He is Jesus Immanuel, God with *us*.

— *Kelley Mathews*

1. Francis Brown, S. R. Driver, and Charles A. Briggs, *The Brown-Driver-Briggs Hebrew and English Lexicon* (Peabody, Mass.: Hendrickson, 2006), 761.
2. Frederick William Danker, ed., *A Greek-English Lexicon of the New Testament and other Early Christian Literature*, 3rd ed. (Chicago: University of Chicago Press, 2000), 777.

CHRIST

Christ is the Greek translation of the Hebrew word *Messiah*, which means "the Anointed One." [1] The name denotes that Jesus was sent by God, set apart for His great redemptive work that was anticipated in the Old Testament.

We see that anticipation in Peter's reply when Jesus asked, "Who do you say that I am?" (Matthew 16:15). Peter answered, "You are the Christ, the Son of the living God" (16:16). Peter's response was rooted in this expectation of the Messiah — a hope that went back to Abraham, who was given a promise that all nations would be blessed through his seed (Genesis 12:1–3; Galatians 3:14–16). Then finally, there Messiah was, in the flesh, talking with Peter and the other disciples.

In that moment, Peter did more than simply identify Jesus. The disciple equated the Christ with the living Son of God,

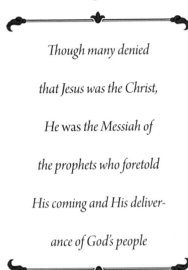

Though many denied

that Jesus was the Christ,

He was the Messiah of

the prophets who foretold

His coming and His deliver-

ance of God's people

recognizing that Jesus was the one chosen by God. We see this affirmed at Jesus' baptism when a voice from heaven declared, "This is My beloved Son, in whom I am well-pleased" (Matthew 3:17). The one sent and consecrated by God was God Himself, who took on flesh to rescue us.

Imagine what it must have felt like to have the person Peter had been waiting for right there with him! Though many denied that Jesus was the Christ, He *was* the Messiah of the prophets who foretold His coming and His deliverance of God's people.

To believe that "Jesus is the Christ" is to believe that He was sent by God to redeem humankind and to rule as Israel's King. Interestingly, though, Jesus used many names to let people know He was the Messiah, but He never used the word *Messiah* or *Christ*.[2] That makes His response to Peter all the more remarkable: "Blessed are you, Simon Barjona, because flesh and blood did not reveal this to you, but My Father who is in heaven" (16:17).

How did Peter know that Jesus was the Christ? Because God revealed it to him! Peter had waited so long for the Messiah, believing He would offer God's kingdom to Israel. But Peter didn't know when the Messiah would arrive. And he had no idea just how much it would impact him. Imagine the thrill of having his eyes opened to Jesus the Christ!

Like Peter, we live in a world of expectation. All around us, people hope for something better. Unlike Peter, we don't have to wait for the Messiah. Jesus the Christ already arrived.

Since He first set foot on earth, Jesus has been thought of in many ways. For some, He is simply a prophet, a teacher, or a rebel. As with Peter, it takes the work of God to reveal to us that Jesus is the Christ. To believe that Jesus is the Christ is to believe that God sent Him as both king and redeemer to His people.

As believers, we can confess that Jesus is the Christ because our eyes have been opened to the truth of the gospel. May we be patient with those who cannot yet see who Jesus is, and may the Holy Spirit help us explain to them that Jesus is the anticipated and foretold hope for us all. He is what our hearts long for — something better, something different, a brand-new life. May this truth give us hope for today and for His return when He will set everything right.

— *Lisa Robinson*

1.   Donald Juel, "Christ," in *Eerdmans Dictionary of the Bible*, ed. David Noel Freedman and others (Grand Rapids: Eerdmans, 2000), 236.
2.   R. T. France, "Messiah," in *New Bible Dictionary*, 2nd ed., ed. J. D. Douglas and others (Downers Grove, Ill.: InterVarsity Press, 1982), 770.

CHAPTER:VERSE

SERVANT

"The Son of Man

did not come

to be served,

but to serve,

and to give

His life a ransom

for many."

— Matthew 20:28

When Matthew picked up his pen and began his biography — his gospel — of Jesus Christ, he hoped to prove to his fellow Jews that Jesus was the long anticipated Messiah (the Christ). To do that, however, he needed to explain why the Messiah didn't come as a conquering king, as the Jews supposed He would, but instead as a suffering servant.

Part of Matthew's explanation came in quoting the "prince" of the prophets, Isaiah, who foresaw the coming of the messianic servant (Isaiah 42:1–4; Matthew 12:18–21). According to Isaiah (and Matthew), the Servant-Messiah would be filled with the Spirit (Isaiah 42:1; Matthew 12:18), gentle and humble (Isaiah 42:2; Matthew 12:19), compassionate (Isaiah 42:3; Matthew 12:20), just (Isaiah 42:1, 3 – 4; Matthew 12:18, 20), and steadfast (Isaiah 42:4; Matthew 12:21).

These terms describe Jesus perfectly. But Jesus' own descriptions of Himself are just as compelling. Jesus' favorite *name* for Himself in Matthew's gospel was "Son of Man" — a messianic title found in Daniel 7:13 – 14. Jesus' favorite *title* for Himself was "servant." Jesus fused the two together in His greatest declaration of purpose: "The Son of Man did not come to be served, but to serve" (Matthew 20:28).

As a *diakonos* — one who volunteers for service to help others — Jesus' greatest illustration of service came when He wore the apron of humility. Though existing in eternity past in the "form of God," Jesus took on the "form of a bond-servant" (Philippians 2:6 – 7). And just hours before His condemnation and death on a cross, Jesus tied a towel about His waist and washed His disciples' feet (John 13:4 – 11).

A faithful servant to God the Father, Jesus acted according to the Father's will alone (Matthew 26:39; Mark 14:36; Luke 22:41 – 42; John 5:19, 30), committing Himself to finishing the task set before Him. And though others tried to dissuade Him (Matthew 16:22 – 23), He chose to "stedfastly set His face [like a flint] to go to Jerusalem" (Luke 9:51 KJV) to accomplish the greatest demonstration of

A faithful servant to

God the Father,

Jesus acted according to

the Father's will alone

service known to humanity: "to give His life [as] a ransom for many" (Matthew 20:28).

Jesus offered Himself, to the Jews first, as the Servant-Messiah, in fulfillment of Old Testament prophecy and promise (Isaiah 42:1; 49:6 – 7; 52:13; 53:11; Romans 15:8). But the

Jews "disowned" God's servant, the "Holy and Righteous One," the "Prince of life" (Acts 3:13–15). Then, the Servant-Messiah offered Himself to the Gentiles in an act of divine mercy, as shown ultimately on the cross — all as a means to glorify God (Romans 15:9). It is for the glory of God that Jesus came among us as our servant (Luke 22:27).

It is also for this reason that we, the servants of the Servant-Messiah, must serve one another, "devoted to one another in brotherly love; [giving] preference to one another in honor; not lagging behind in diligence, [being] fervent in spirit, serving the Lord" (Romans 12:10–11). But our motivation for service ought not to be for the public acclaim often received in serving in high-profile roles — such as preachers and teachers or elders and deacons. These are godly, necessary acts of service; however, our motivation for service (no matter which area of service) should carry an attitude of silent humility. We must humbly serve widows and orphans (James 1:27), the homeless, prostitutes, addicts of various kinds, those with special needs (both mental and physical), those in the nursery, and the elderly — in the same manner in which Jesus humbly served.

And if we demonstrate the same love and devotion as our Servant-Messiah, then one day we will hear the greatest commendation anyone could receive: "Well done, good and faithful servant!" (Matthew 25:21, 23 NIV).

— *Derrick G. Jeter*

KING

We read in the Old Testament that God established kings over His people. This wasn't anything new. Kings and kingdoms were prevalent in ancient Near East culture. Kings were rulers of their nations and spoke with absolute authority over their people regions. Kings laid down the law and dared anyone to disobey. Is it any wonder that in some nations, the king had a god-like status?

But God had a different, intended purpose for the kings He appointed — to show through them that He was the real ruler. How were these kings to accomplish this? By upholding God's justice and rule for Israel, by proclaiming the law, and by preserving righteousness — which they did as long as they esteemed God as King and listened to His prophets (1 Kings 3:28).

Even initially when the Israelites desired a human king for wrong motives, establishing an earthly kingship over them had been in God's game plan all along (Deuteronomy 17:15; 1 Samuel 8:4–5). He promised an eternal King, who would sit on the throne of David forever (2 Samuel 7:12–13).

The problem was God's kings didn't glorify Him as intended until the eternal King arrived. The kings went bad, and eventually, the Israelites lost possession

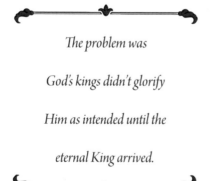

The problem was

God's kings didn't glorify

Him as intended until the

eternal King arrived.

of their land and the privilege of having a human representative. As

they anticipated restoration of the kingdom, the Israelites believed that God's promised eternal King would be merely a warrior with an army who would overthrow Rome and reestablish an earthly throne. When Jesus finally arrived, He didn't fit that bill in the eyes of many, most notably the religious leaders who questioned Him, mocked Him, and eventually turned Him over to Rome. Even at Jesus' death on the cross, the mockers ridiculed the notion that He claimed to be king and yet He couldn't even save Himself (Matthew 27:42).

Where the people expected a valiant warrior who would overturn Roman rule and recapture the land for Israel, Jesus showed the people something different. He affirmed Old Testament prophecy; He was the one to bring justice for the subjects of the kingdom. And although Jesus offered Israel the literal, long-awaited kingdom of God on earth, His kingdom was not *of* this world. His justice would come, not by way of a military coup but by reconciliation with the Father and a restored relationship with Him. Those who believed in Jesus embraced His kingship. Those who did not mocked and ridiculed Him.

People are no different today. They easily understand the concept of an earthly king yet struggle to recognize Christ as the sovereign ruler who will judge the world of sin. In their unbelief, they sneer and mock. They wonder why our King doesn't right wrongs. As Christians, we may wonder how it is that Jesus is the king when justice and peace are so elusive, both in our personal lives and in the world around us. It helps to remember what the writer of Hebrews proclaimed about Christ: "But of the Son, He says, 'Your throne, O God, is forever and ever, and the righteous scepter is the scepter of His kingdom'" (Hebrews 1:8).

What does that mean for us? We can look ahead with hope, knowing that there will come a day when He will reign over His earthly kingdom (1 Timothy 6:15; Revelation 19:16). He will rule openly and bring swift justice to those who mocked Him and would not believe in Him (Matthew 25:41–46).

Let us hide that hope in our hearts when we get discouraged at the injustices we see. When the world ridicules, let us keep in our minds that Christ will come again to reign, and let that reality influence the way we live. He promises justice and peace and, one day, He will set everything right.

— *Lisa Robinson*

RABBI

When you need your eyes checked, you go to an optometrist. When your house needs rewiring, you call a certified electrician. In the first century, when the Jews needed teaching from the Law, they sought out experts too — men known as rabbis.

The terms *rabbi* and *rabboni* were respectfully given to well-read teachers of Mosaic Law, the Prophets, and the Midrash (Jewish commentaries).[1] In the first century, with no temple or priests, Jews gathered in synagogues to listen to and learn from rabbis.

In Jesus' time, rabbis represented the diversity of Jewish communities of the Diaspora. Some were Pharisees, who were descendants of tradesmen and had become experts at interpreting rabbinic oral tradition. Others were Sadducees — descendants of Levites, the priestly tribe of Israel. Sadducees held the reputation of strictly adhering to the Torah. This group also rejected belief in the afterlife.[2]

Jesus — a poor carpenter from Nazareth whom many had begun to call Rabbi — stood in stark contrast to both groups, demonstrating an unmatched ability to interpret Scripture, even as a boy (Luke 2:46 – 47). Jesus taught with mastery about everything from the afterlife to the Sabbath and, unlike the Pharisees and Sadducees, demonstrated compassion for the poor and the voiceless.

Naturally, Jesus piqued the interest of the religious leaders, but eventually, their curiosity soured into jealousy and malice. The Pharisees and Sadducees had long been treated with esteem and wielded great power over the people. Then Jesus came along and instead of esteeming those Israel regarded as experts, He chided them:

> "They love the place of honor at banquets and the chief seats in the synagogues, and respectful greetings in the market places, and being called Rabbi by men. But do not be called Rabbi; for One is your Teacher, and you are all brothers." (Matthew 23:6 – 8)

Jesus understood that the people's so-called rabbis majored in hypocrisy and entitlement and minored in the heart of God. Where Yahweh provided the Law out of a desire for His people to

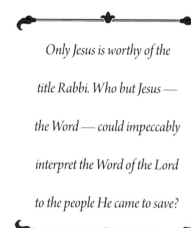

Only Jesus is worthy of the title Rabbi. Who but Jesus — the Word — could impeccably interpret the Word of the Lord to the people He came to save?

be set apart and remain devoted to Him, the religious leaders used rules about hand washing and the Sabbath to condemn those they considered less important . . . including Jesus.

Ironically, He was the only one who deserved to be called rabbi — the One Teacher sent from the Father. The Bible attests to this, as *rabbi* and *rabboni* are used seventeen times in the New Testament, and fourteen of those are references to Jesus.

Today, we don't use names like Pharisee or Sadducee, but our world isn't free of those climbing the ladder of religious esteem. It's easy to fall prey to the cult of personality — to align ourselves with one preacher or writer over others, elevating that person to star-status and denigrating other Christians who differ on non-essential issues. (See how Paul speaks against this in 1 Corinthians 1:10–17.)

It's tempting to get carried away with righteous indignation when political and social circumstances veer from godliness to the profane. But God doesn't call us to create hierarchies of righteousness. Rather, we're called to tell the story of God's love, remembering that we, too, are recipients of His grace and mercy.

Only Jesus is worthy of the title Rabbi. Who but Jesus — the Word — could impeccably interpret the Word of the Lord to the people He came to save? His teaching is a conduit of God's grace. God didn't *have* to interpret Himself to us. He didn't *need* to send His Son to become a man — tempted, hungry, scourged, and murdered — to explain to us His holiness and boundless love. But He did!

In response, let's stay humble and incline our hearts to the only One and Only Rabbi.

— *Sharifa Stevens*

1. "Jews in New Testament Times," in *Illustrated Manners and Customs of the Bible*, ed. J. I. Packer and Merrill C. Tenney (Nashville: Thomas Nelson, 1980), 502.
2. "Jews in New Testament Times," ed. Packer and Tenney, 506.

SON OF MAN

And He began to

teach them that

the Son of Man must

suffer many things

and be rejected by the

elders and the chief priests

and the scribes,

and be killed, and

after three days

rise again.

— Mark 8:31

The name "son of man" can be found in both the Old and New Testaments. In the Old Testament, God addressed the prophet Ezekiel as "son of man" more than eighty times. (Ezekiel 2:1 is the first of many.) The prophets also used "son of man" while communicating the word of the Lord to indicate the temporal, fleeting nature of humanity (Isaiah 51:12; Jeremiah 49:33).

The New Testament presents a shift in which "Son of Man" refers exclusively to Jesus. Jesus referred to Himself as the Son of Man more than seventy-five times in the New Testament — most likely making the name His favorite self-designation.[1] Why did He use it so often? *To illustrate the fulfillment of prophecy as found in Daniel 7:13 –14.*

In Matthew 24, Jesus taught His disciples to watch for signs of the end of the age. While explaining His return after His death, resurrection, and ascension, Jesus quoted Daniel 7:13, saying:

> "Then the sign of the Son of Man will appear in the sky, and then all the tribes of the earth will mourn, and they will see the Son of Man coming on the clouds of the sky with power and great glory." (Matthew 24:30)

In Luke 22:69, Jesus again alluded to Daniel 7, along with Psalm 110:1, this time in response to the Sanhedrin, right before His execution. The members of the Sanhedrin immediately understood what Jesus meant and, suspecting blasphemy, angrily asked if He was the Son of God.

In addition to establishing Himself as the fulfillment of prophecy, Jesus referred to Himself as the Son of Man *to remind listeners (and readers)* of the marvel of the hypostatic union. ("Hypostatic union" means that Jesus has two distinct

The Son of Man

is the flawless

representative of

humanity.

natures — human and divine — existing in one Person. He is fully man and fully God.) Colossians 2:9 says, "For in Him all the fullness of Deity dwells in bodily form." In other words, Jesus is fully *God* — the second person of the Trinity who exists eternally and through whom all things originate. But he is also fully *human* — having been born, tempted, hungry, angry, and ultimately put to death.

The Son of Man is the flawless representative of humanity. He is the second Adam (1 Corinthians 15:21–22), redeeming humankind by becoming a man. Adam was the first human, and he and Eve brought sin and death into the world. Jesus is the triumphant *answer* to sin and death; His life and death atone for the sins of all who believe in Him, and His resurrection is a promise of eternal life for all who put their trust in Him. Where Adam brought death, Jesus brings life.

As the Son of Man, Jesus embodies the tension of choosing to be confined to humanity and yet having the authority and power of heaven. He emptied Himself (Philippians 2:7) in order to fulfill His sacrificial and salvific duties as Messiah. Thus, in Luke 9:22, Jesus said:

"The Son of Man must suffer many things and be rejected by the elders and chief priests and scribes, and be killed and be raised up on the third day."

Because Jesus *did* suffer, *did* die, and *did* rise on the third day, we have in Him a powerful advocate. To save us, the Son of Man left His heavenly glory to become a man and gave Himself up to be mocked, scourged, and murdered. And His commitment to being fully man is eternal — when we meet the Son of Man, we will be able to hug Him, see His eyes smile, and share a cluster of grapes. And we will know in Him a love as deep as the scars He bears.

— *Sharifa Stevens*

1. James Oliver Buswell, Jr., "Son of Man," in *Zondervan's Pictorial Bible Dictionary*, gen. ed. Merrill C. Tenney (Grand Rapids: Zondervan, 1967), 805.

SON OF DAVID

When he heard

that it was Jesus the

Nazarene, he began

to cry out and say,

"Jesus, Son of David,

have mercy on me!"

— Mark 10:47

Bartimaeus may have been blind, but he correctly perceived Jesus as the "Son of David." The sightless man's plea for healing revealed his hope that Jesus was the promised Messiah who would rule with the power of God. That hope did not disappoint; Jesus healed Bartimaeus on that dusty Jericho roadside.

The name Son of David holds both literal and prophetic meaning. According to the genealogies in Matthew 1 and Luke 3, Jesus, through Joseph, was a direct descendant of David. Moreover, in Acts 13:23, Paul attested to Jesus as *the* Son of David when the apostle addressed the Jews in Antioch, saying, "From the descendants of this man [David], according to promise, God has brought to Israel a Savior, Jesus."

What was the "promise" Paul referred to? The answer lies in 2 Samuel 7:12–16, a pivotal passage known as the Davidic Covenant. With this covenant, the Lord promised to honor King David's desire to build a house for Him, to protect David's dynasty, and to give his descendants favor forever.

God's faithfulness to this covenant shone — He blessed David's son Solomon as he assumed the throne. Solomon responded by building a temple dedicated to God (2 Chronicles 7:11–16). As

But like Bartimaeus,

we can have faith that the

Son of David hears our cries

and can heal us.

Israel's ruler, he possessed otherworldly wisdom, and his kingdom prospered (1 Kings 4:20–34). Unfortunately, Solomon failed to remain faithful to God.

First Kings 11 records Solomon's idolatry and God's response — to rip the kingdom from Solomon's son. The forever-kingdom seemed impossible.

But with God, nothing is impossible.

Ultimately, God fulfilled the Davidic Covenant through His Son, Jesus. Jesus, too, built a dwelling place for God — a temple of which He is the Cornerstone (Ephesians 2:20–22). And because Jesus is fully God as well as fully man (Colossians 1:15–17), His rule is everlasting.

A *major* sign that the messianic Son of David had arrived was His ability to cast out demons, give sight to the blind, and heal the sick — a fulfillment of the prophet's words in Isaiah 29:18–19. Observe the passages where Jesus is referred to as "Son of David" and you'll discover a pattern. Blind Bartimaeus in Mark 10:46–52, the Canaanite woman with the demoniac daughter in Matthew 15:21–28, the two blind men in Matthew 20:30 – 34 — everyone who used that title for Jesus either experienced supernatural healing or witnessed it by His hand.

Death, failed relationships, miscarriage, illness — this world leaves us blinded by tragedy, arms outstretched, desperate for God's intervention in our lives. But like Bartimaeus, we can have faith that the Son of David hears our cries and can heal us. Even now, Jesus is seated at the right hand of the Father (Hebrews 1:3), which means that when we shout, "Have mercy on me, Son of David!" we have audience with the King.

The favor of the Son of David extends to *anyone* who trusts in Him. The house of God, formerly human-made and vulnerable to ruin, is now indestructible. Solomon sinned and his kingdom suffered for it. Jesus knew temptation, yet did not sin, and His kingdom benefits from His flawlessness. Solomon died and was buried. Jesus died and rose again — He will *never* abandon His throne, *never* mislead His people, and *never* again die.

— *Sharifa Stevens*

MASTER

Jesus' disciples called Him Master, a fact Luke took special note of in his gospel account. Master is an especially poetic title for Jesus for two reasons. First, it was often used synonymously with *teacher*, which aptly describes a large portion of Jesus' public ministry (Matthew 11:1; Mark 6:34).

Secondly, the Hebrew word for "master" or "lord" is *adon* or *adonai*.[1] While the Hebrew term was used commonly to connote household or political authority (Genesis 45:8), it was also frequently used as a name for God. Reverent Jews today still say *adonai* in place of *YHWH*, or Yahweh, which they consider too sacred to utter.

To call Jesus Master was not just a sign of respect but also an inspired nod to His *deity.* Luke, in writing his gospel account, acknowledged this by using the term to describe Jesus' divine authority over creation, perhaps most memorably in the accounts of the Lord's interaction with water and the sick.

Take Luke 5 for example. One day as Jesus was teaching near the Sea of Galilee, He spotted two abandoned boats. Jesus got into one of them to continue teaching the large crowd. Earlier that day, Peter had been fishing on the same boat for hours and had not caught a thing. Jesus directed him to set out a bit from the shore and cast his nets just one more time. Peter responded, "Master, we worked hard all night and caught nothing, but I will do as You say and let down the nets" (Luke 5:5). Suddenly, Peter's nets couldn't contain the large number of fish he scooped out of the water. Two boats and several fishermen later, Peter was still struggling not to sink under the weight of fish (5:6–7)!

Three chapters later, in Luke 8:22–25, the chaotic and mysterious water once again played counterpoint to Jesus' mastery. The disciples and Jesus embarked to sail from one side of the lake to the other. Jesus fell asleep, and a storm ensued. The boat began to take on water, and terrified, the disciples turned to slumbering Jesus and screamed, "Master, Master, we are perishing!" With a word, Jesus calmed the wind and the waves. Astonished and scared, the disciples wondered, *Who is this?*

Between Luke 5 and 8, *because of the word or touch of Jesus,* fish gave themselves to be caught; the waves surrendered; people were healed of leprosy (5:13); the lame began to walk (5:24–25); a man's withered hand was made whole (6:10); and a centurion's servant was delivered from fatal illness (7:6–10). A mother's son even rose from the dead (7:12–15)!

The disciples witnessed these things with their own eyes. They rightly called Jesus Master, but they *still wondered who He was.*[2]

They're not alone. Today, even with the biblical testimony of Jesus' mastery over creation, we

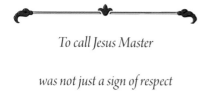

To call Jesus Master

was not just a sign of respect

but also an inspired nod

to His deity.

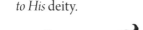

call out to Him without expecting much. He has done the impossible by reconciling us to God, forgiving our sins, and conquering death — because He is Master over the spiritual *and* the physical — but we still don't get who He is.

Jesus — the Master — is in control. He is as powerful today as He was when He walked the earth. He has dominion over the wind and waves of our lives. We can come to Him with our empty nets, our stormy journeys, our lives drenched with troubles, confident in His compassion and ability to save us.

— *Sharifa Stevens*

1. *Zondervan's Pictorial Bible Dictionary*, gen. ed. Merrill C. Tenney (Grand Rapids: Zondervan, 1967), 515.
2. Walter L. Liefeld, "Luke," in *The Expositor's Commentary — Abridged Edition: New Testament*, ed. Kenneth L. Barker and John R. Kohlenberger III (Grand Rapids: Zondervan, 1994), 239.

THE WORD

In the beginning
was the Word, and
the Word was
with God, and the
Word was God.

— John 1:1

Have you ever been in an argument with your best friend or spouse that ended in the silent treatment? Hours pass like days in that kind of icy distance.

Now, imagine *four hundred years* of silence.

God freed Israel from bondage in Egypt and caused the nation to take possession of the Promised Land. But the people were not faithful. To warn Israel of coming punishment, God sent prophets who preceded their prophecies with the phrase, "The *word* of the Lord." The prophets begged Israel to listen, but Israel turned a deaf ear. Systemic idolatry eroded the relationship between God and Israel, resulting in a fractured kingdom and, ultimately, exile from and foreign occupation of the Promised Land. Malachi was the last prophet to speak.

And then ... silence.

Then, like drops of rain seeping into parched earth, the Word quenched the dusty silence of four hundred years.

God *spoke* — not through a new prophet but through His very Son, Jesus Christ, the Word! The author of Hebrews wrote, "God, after He spoke long ago to the fathers in the prophets in many portions and in many ways, *in these last days has spoken to us in His Son*, whom He appointed heir of all things, through whom also He made the world" (Hebrews 1:1–2, emphasis added).

John, in his gospel account, his first epistle, and the book of Revelation, described Jesus as the Word, or *Logos* in Greek, so that his readers — from devout Jews who knew the Genesis creation account to Gentile students of Greek cosmology[1] — would believe in Jesus as God the Son, the focal point of all creation.

The *Word is associated with truth*. Even today, when people want to assure others of their sincerity in completing future tasks, they'll say, "I give you my *word*." Jesus' very life is evidence that God keeps His word.

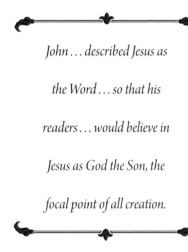

John ... described Jesus as

the Word ... so that his

readers ... would believe in

Jesus as God the Son, the

focal point of all creation.

For example, God makes good on Old Testament prophecies concerning His Son, Jesus, the Messiah: He was born in Bethlehem (Micah 5:2) of a virgin (Isaiah 7:14), His lineage was of the tribe of Judah (Genesis 49:10), He was crucified (Zechariah 12:10), and He rose again (Psalm 49:15). Jesus fulfilled hundreds of prophecies concerning the Messiah, as recorded by several psalmists and prophets united by one foundation: the Word of the Lord.

The Word is associated with creation. In the first chapter of John, the apostle mirrored the Genesis 1 account, pulling back the curtain on *who* was there in the beginning:

> In the beginning was the Word, and the Word was with God, and the Word was God. He was in the beginning with God. All things came into being through Him, and apart from Him nothing came into being that has come into being. (John 1:1–3)

These three verses are densely packed with theology, asserting that Jesus is *eternal*. He was *present* at the beginning of time, and because He is timeless, He's without beginning or end. Jesus was not only present with God, but He *is* God. Jesus is the *active Creator* — the catalyst, the artist, the first cause of creation. He made it all (Colossians 1:16–17). There is a beautiful symmetry between the Genesis account, where God said, "Let there be light," and John 1, in which Jesus is called *the Word*. Jesus is both the fulfillment of Old Testament prophecy and the one responsible for the way creation came to be.

John 1:14 states that the Word "became flesh" and dwelled with us. He who was immortal took on mortal flesh, condescended to leave His throne in glory — to be with us. In essence, He became a man to be Immanuel — "God with us" — so that through Him, we could *read* God's heart, not from His prophets but directly from His Son, the *Word*.

— *Sharifa Stevens*

1. Heraclitus, a Greek philosopher, proposed that the *Logos* was that which connected humanity with the divine and the universe. *Logos* was the natural law. H. Kleinknecht, "The Logos in the Greek and Hellenistic World" in *The Theological Dictionary of the New Testament*, ed. Gerhard Kittel and Gerhard Friedrich, trans. Geoffrey W. Bromiley (Grand Rapids: Eerdmans, 1992), 506.

LAMB OF GOD

The next day he saw
Jesus coming to him
and said, "Behold, the
Lamb of God who
takes away the
sin of the world!" …
and he looked at
Jesus as He walked,
and said, "Behold,
the Lamb of God!"

— John 1:29, 36

None came more sharp-edged than John the Baptizer — not Jonah with his acid-stained skin, not Hosea with his perpetually unfaithful wife, and certainly not Jeremiah with his ceaseless weeping. John was the last of the "Thus saith the Lord," fire-and-brimstone-like prophets. He lived a hard life in the uncivilized wilderness of Judea, wearing camel-hair clothes and eating bugs and honey (Matthew 3:1, 4). And he preached a hard message: "Repent, for the kingdom of heaven is at hand" (3:2).

But when John saw Jesus, everything changed — everything he'd hoped for was fulfilled. The object of his message had come.

The question in the Old Testament is "Where is the lamb?" (Genesis 22:7). The answer in the New Testament is "Behold, the Lamb of God who takes away the sin of the world!" (John 1:29).

On the eve of the Israelites' deliverance from slavery in Egypt, God commanded the children of Israel to sacrifice an unblemished, year-old male lamb and to spread its blood on the lintels and doorposts of their houses (Exodus 12:1–13, 21–22). "The destroyer" (death) then descended upon Egypt killing all firstborn men and animals — except for those whose houses were marked by the blood of a lamb (12:23).

From that day, until the destruction of the temple in Jerusalem in AD 70, Jews sacrificed a Passover lamb in celebration of their salvation from Egyptian bondage. So, when John pointed to Jesus and said, "Behold, the Lamb of God" (John 1:36), he declared the appearance of God's means of salvation from sin and death.

John proclaimed Jesus' sacrifice would take away the totality of the world's sin — not just an individual's acts of sin but *all* sin — and that no sin is beyond the sacrificial atonement of God's Lamb.

Sacrificial lambs were offered yearly at Passover, because no lamb could be offered once for all as atonement for a lifetime of humanity's sin (Hebrews 10:1–4). Yet, the Lamb of God was more than sufficient to be offered once for all, taking away the sin of the world for all time (7:27; 10:10). How could that be? How could Jesus' one-time sacrifice take away worldwide sin forever . . . when the untold millions of Passover lambs that had been sacrificed over a millennia couldn't permanently take away the sin of the Jews?

Even if Jesus' innocence, meekness, and sacrifice merited the name "Lamb," as a *mere man*, His blood wouldn't be sufficient to remove humanity's sin any more than an innocent and unblemished lamb could remove the Jews' sin. But Jesus wasn't (and isn't) a mere man — He is the God-Man, the Son of God, the eternal Word. The apostle John made it clear that at the beginning of time "the Word" existed "with God" and "was God" (John 1:1), and this divine Word took on human flesh and "dwelt among us" (1:14). It was this divine-human, this

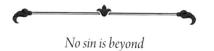

No sin is beyond

the sacrificial atonement

of God's Lamb.

God-Man, of whom John the Baptizer testified (1:15), saying: "Behold, the Lamb of God who takes away the sin of the world!" (1:29).

Jesus is not merely the Lamb ordained and sent by God, but He is the Lamb who is God. When He poured out His blood, it wasn't merely the physical properties of plasma, red blood cells, white blood cells, and platelets that stained the cross and streaked His face and body. It was natural, human blood infused with supernatural, divine mercy and grace — which together in Christ alone provides the power to remove sin.

It was human blood coursing through the veins of the divine Lamb whose sacrificial death on the cross bought us from the slave market of sin (Acts 20:28). And because He paid such a great price to give such a great gift, we join the heavenly choir and sing:

"Worthy is the Lamb that was slain to receive power and riches and wisdom and might and honor and glory and blessing." (Revelation 5:12)

— *Derrick G. Jeter*

MESSIAH

Messiah is the transliteration of the Hebrew word *mashiah*, which means "anointed one" in Hebrew. *Christos*, or "Christ," is the Greek word often used in place of *Messiah*.[1]

In Old Testament times, people and things chosen by God to fulfill a specific purpose were often anointed by having oil poured over them. For example, the tabernacle was anointed before it was used (Exodus 40:9–11), and priests were anointed (Leviticus 8:30). The same was true of Israel's kings, who were set apart as "the Lord's anointed."[2] Scripture features this idea in several places. David spared Saul's life because Saul was "the LORD's anointed" (1 Samuel 24:6). David referred to himself as "anointed of the God of Jacob" in 2 Samuel 23:1. And in a unique instance, the prophet Isaiah referred to a foreign king — Cyrus of Persia — as the Lord's "anointed" in Isaiah 45:1, demonstrating God's universal authority to install rulers (Daniel 2:21).

After King Solomon's death, the kingdom of Israel split (1 Kings 12:16–17), the Assyrians carried the people of Israel away into exile (2 Kings 24:14; 25:11; 1 Chronicles 5:26), and prophecies hushed. The Israelites were left with Malachi's words ringing in their ears:

> "Behold, I am going to send My messenger, and he will clear the way before Me. And the Lord, whom you seek, will suddenly come to His temple; and the messenger of the covenant, in whom you delight, behold, He is coming," says the LORD of hosts. (Malachi 3:1)

During the time between the last prophecy and the birth of Jesus, the definition of *Messiah* came into narrow focus. Messiah would not just be any anointed one. He would be *the* One — a single descendant of David who would return the people to the land of Israel, where He would rule righteously and reconcile the people to God. According to Malachi 3, Messiah would be preceded by "the messenger,"

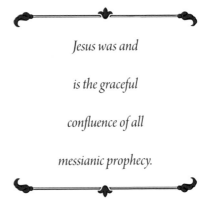

Jesus was and

is the graceful

confluence of all

messianic prophecy.

whom Malachi later identified as Elijah (Malachi 4:5). (See also the Levites' discourse with John the Baptist in John 1:19–27.)

During the time between the Old and New Testaments, religious experts crystallized the profile of the Messiah by combing through Scripture. Messiah would be the Suffering Servant (Isaiah 53), given dominion over all by the Ancient of Days

(Daniel 7:13–14). He would be of the tribe of Judah (Genesis 49:10). He would bring prosperity (Amos 9:13) and peace (Isaiah 32:1–8). Messiah would usher in freedom and proclaim the favorable year of the Lord (61:1–2).

After Jesus arrived, He didn't publicly declare, "I am the Messiah!" His works testified to His title, and Jesus didn't come to gain political power or favor from religious elites but to be the Savior of sinners (Mark 2:17). In fact, the closest Jesus came to such a declaration was not before the religious experts of His day, but at a solitary well with a Samaritan woman, who responded by believing in Him and sharing her faith (John 4:26, 42).

Jesus was and is the graceful confluence of all messianic prophecy. And yet, when He stood before the religious experts who accused Him of blasphemy on the night before His crucifixion, they didn't recognize Him. More than anyone, they should have known, but they sent the One they had long awaited to His death.

Chances are, Jesus isn't going to materialize on your sofa to declare He is Messiah. He doesn't need to; Scripture already testifies to this truth. We can be like the religious experts, knowing all the passages and seeing the signs but refusing to worship Him, or we can be like the Samaritan woman, who believed and, with humility and excitement, shared the gospel with others.

— *Sharifa Stevens*

1. "Messianic Prophecy and Prophecy in General," in *Old Testament Survey: The Message, Form, and Background of the Old Testament*, 2nd ed., ed. William Sanford LaSor and others (Grand Rapids: Eerdmans, 1996), 689.

BREAD OF LIFE

Forty years. That's a long time to eat the same thing . . . every day. "What's for lunch, honey?" "Quail and manna." "What's for dinner?" "Manna and quail." But for forty years, the children of Israel ate from the same menu—manna cakes, flaming manna soufflé, and bamanna bread (Exodus 16:35). They grumbled about it at the time, but future generations (who didn't have to endure one creative dish of manna after another) saw God's wilderness provision as a miracle.

Perhaps that's why when Jesus fed five thousand men—not counting women and children—from a single, small lunch, the people wanted to make Him king (John 6:15). Jesus' time hadn't come for that, though, so He escaped across the Sea of Galilee. Eventually, the people caught up with Him the next day in Capernaum (John 6:24–25), so Jesus took the opportunity to teach them something about Moses, manna, and the Messiah.

The people who partook of the miracle the day before believed Jesus was the promised Prophet (Deuteronomy 18:15–19; John 6:14), but only because He fed their physical hunger

The Bread of Life —

Jesus — permanently

satisfies our

spiritual hunger.

(John 6:26). Like the Samaritan woman who misunderstood what Jesus meant by "living water" (4:10, 14), the people misunderstood the significance of the miracle of the loaves. They thought He would give them food that would satisfy their physical needs every day they lived on earth (6:34). Not so. Jesus

was offering much more — food that would satisfy their spiritual needs for eternity (6:27). All they needed to do was believe in the One born in Bethlehem, the village known as the "House of Bread."

But the people didn't believe. The hardness of their hearts, despite the miracle they experienced the day before, led them to demand a sign equal to or greater than Moses' miracle (6:30–31).

The Jews expected that the coming Messiah would surpass, or at least replicate, the wilderness miracle. They viewed Moses as the source of the miracle — a power that was bestowed upon him because of his merits and that ended at his death. Jesus corrected their shortsightedness. It wasn't Moses who provided for the Israelites' physical needs; it was God. Jesus reminded the people (and us) of the truth that we must look to God first and foremost when we are in need. More importantly, Jesus turned the discussion back to their spiritual need and to the fact that in Jesus, God had given heavenly bread, which gives eternal life, not just to Israel, but to the whole world (John 6:32 – 33).

Jesus had already said that He didn't come offering a new interpretation of the Law but a fulfillment of the Law (Matthew 5:17). Then, without mincing words, He told the people that the bread which "came down from heaven" (John 6:41, 50 – 51, 58) was He Himself — the Bread of Life (6:35, 48, 51).

Bread temporarily satisfies our physical hunger, but the Bread of Life — Jesus — permanently satisfies our spiritual hunger. Feasting on the Bread of Life — accepting and believing in Jesus — fills our spiritual bellies, sustains and nourishes our spirits, and gratifies our deepest hunger: our desire for eternal life.

Those who've tasted the Bread of Life receive eternal life and the promise from Jesus that they will not go spiritually hungry; they will be accepted by Christ and in no way cast out (6:36 – 40). This is the assurance we have — our salvation is secure because the Bread of Life never spoils and always satisfies.

— *Derrick G. Jeter*

GOOD SHEPHERD

"I am the good shepherd; the good shepherd lays down His life for the sheep.... I am the good shepherd, and I know My own and My own know Me."

— John 10:11, 14

No illustration of the relationship between God and His people is more iconic than that of the shepherd and the sheep . . . which is ironic because throughout Israel's history shepherds occupied one of the lowest rungs in Jewish society. Their occupation required them to live and work outdoors with the sheep, so they were perpetually dirty and, therefore, ceremonially unclean. Yet, Moses, Israel's greatest prophet, and David, Israel's greatest king, were both shepherds when they were charged with caring for God's people (Exodus 3:1, 10; 1 Samuel 16:11–12; 1 Chronicles 11:1–2). Even the promised and long-awaited Messiah, as foretold by the prophet Micah, would be known as Israel's Shepherd (Micah 5:2, 4). But Israel's Shepherd would not be a shepherd of goats and lambs as were His forefathers Moses and

David; rather, He would be the Shepherd of His people.

It was Micah's prophecy the scribes quoted when Herod inquired as to the birthplace of the Messiah (Matthew 2:6). In time, the Messiah identified Himself as Israel's Shepherd, offering to lead the nation away from the barren wasteland of their sinful selfishness and dead religiosity . . . and into the luscious pastureland of salvation found only in a living relationship with the living God. But many in Israel, like wayward sheep, rejected their Shepherd—Jesus. So He gathered other sheep not born to Israel's flock, who also longed for someone to shepherd their souls (1 Peter 2:25).

And whether Jew or Gentile, the New Testament presents the Shepherd of our souls in three different lights, each highlighting a significant theological truth.

Jesus is the Good Shepherd, who redeems. When Jesus used the metaphor of the Good Shepherd to describe Himself (John 10:11),

the sheep He had in mind were not just the children of Israel or those who received Him as Messiah during His life on earth, but a world of sinners ruined by the fall and lost in the wilderness of their own sinfulness. This includes us today. But as the Good Shepherd, Jesus took our iniquity, laying down His life by lying down on the cross (Isaiah 53:6). Having redeemed us by marking us with His own blood that was spilled on the cross, the Good Shepherd knows us and we Him (John 10:14); we hear and recognize His voice because we are the flock of His fold, safe and secure within His eternal sheep pen (10:27–28).

Jesus is the Great Shepherd who was resurrected. Our Shepherd is *good* because He laid down His life for His sheep. However, if Jesus had remained in the grave, we would scatter as harassed and helpless sheep (Matthew 9:36; Mark 6:34). But Jesus rose from the grave! And because He did, the Good Shepherd became the Great Shepherd (Hebrews 13:20), causing us, whether or not we walk through death's valley, to lie down in green pastures beside still and soul-restoring waters (Psalm 23:1–4). Our Great Shepherd — the victor over death's shadow — stands

Our Great Shepherd…

stands guard and

protects us with

His rod and staff.

guard and protects us with His rod and staff. Therefore, we have nothing to fear of enemies or evil or death, for we are the anointed sheep of His pasture (23:4–6).

Jesus is the Chief Shepherd who rewards. Because the Good Shepherd redeemed His sheep and because the Great Shepherd, through the power of His resurrection, gives them hope, the Chief Shepherd encourages those with the responsibility to "care for [His] flock" to "watch over" them "willingly, not grudgingly" (1 Peter 5:2 NLT). If these under-shepherds — pastors, teachers, and elders — serve the flock well, then the Chief Shepherd, when He comes for His own at the rapture, will reward them with an unfading glory (5:4).

Sheep are by nature timid, but we have nothing to fear. We are secure in the Good Shepherd's fold. We are protected under the Great Shepherd's rod. And, if we serve God's people, we are rewarded by the Chief Shepherd's hand.

— Derrick G. Jeter

SON OF GOD

In New Testament times, every devout Jew knew Deuteronomy 6:4, the *shema*: "Hear, O Israel! The LORD is our God, the LORD is One!" Oppressed under Roman occupation and without the voice of a prophet to give a new word from the Lord, Jews were daily reminded of the consequences of their past idolatry — the reason they had been cut off from God's blessing and protection (Deuteronomy 28:33 – 37).

If the Jews had learned one thing from the Law, the Prophets, and experience, it was that there was only one true God. They would never stray from this truth again.

Jesus made claims that overturned everything the Jews — especially the religious leaders — thought they knew. He revealed truth within familiar passages of Scripture, but more important, Jesus asserted that He and the Father are one (John 10:30) and that He is the Son of God (Matthew 27:43).

Jewish experts of the Law and the Prophets were familiar with the term "son of God," because the Old Testament utilizes the term a handful of times to describe either the line of Seth (Genesis 6:2, 4) or angels (Job 1:6; 2:1). In those contexts, scholars surmise that "son of God" was meant either as an honorable term (as in Matthew 5:9) or as a synonym for a heavenly being.

The scribes and Pharisees recognized that when Jesus said He was *one* with God *and* called Himself God's "Son," He was claiming *equality* with God — which is why they so often responded to Him with murderous rage (Matthew 26:3–4; John 5:18; 8:57–59). To add to this, Jesus did not meet the Law experts' expectations of how the Son of God was to operate: Why would the so-called Son of God

come so humbly, giving Himself over to humiliation and death? Where was the warrior, the conquering King, the One who would deliver the Jews militarily from Roman oppression?

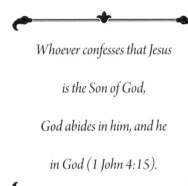

Whoever confesses that Jesus

is the Son of God,

God abides in him, and he

in God (1 John 4:15).

In contrast to the experts of the Law, the Gospels provide examples of others who — through faith — proclaimed Jesus as Son of God: John the Baptist (John 1:34) and the disciple Nathanael (1:49) both recognized through the power of the Holy Spirit that Jesus is the Son of God. A centurion, who presumably had witnessed hundreds of deaths, exclaimed after watching Jesus die, "Truly this man was the Son of God!" (Matthew 27:54; Mark 15:39).

Interestingly, Satan and his demons were *compelled* to properly address Jesus when they encountered Him. They knew Jesus was the Son of God, without equivocation. Satan used the term while tempting Jesus to use His heavenly power on earth (Matthew 4:3, 6; Luke 4:3, 9). Demons shouted the title in fear, knowing that the Son of God is their Lord and Judge (Matthew 8:29; Mark 3:11; Luke 4:41).

But the Son of God requires more than mere acknowledgment of His title (the demons do this, and they are condemned). He asks that we have the faith to abide in Him — to trust Him, though the enemy might try to break us through temptation, suffering, and death.

The books of John and 1 John use the title "Son of God" as part of a confession of *faith*: "Whoever confesses that Jesus is the Son of God, God abides in him, and he in God" (1 John 4:15). Jesus' rule is radical: pardon in place of just punishment, salvation through belief in Him, freedom from works-based fear. His grace is out of this world!

— *Sharifa Stevens*

RESURRECTION AND LIFE

"I am the resurrection and the life; he who believes in Me will live even if he dies."

— John 11:25

Death is an enemy. It is never an ally of God or His creation. And yet, God, at the beginning of human history, pronounced death upon humanity as a just punishment for its vile sin, but He made this pronouncement with a broken heart (Genesis 2:17; 3:19).

In Scripture, death is always referred to in two ways: physical and spiritual. Physical death is the separation of the body from the soul. Spiritual death is the eternal separation of the soul from God. And without Christ, both definitions of death leave a hollow hopelessness in this life and in the life to come. That's why Jesus' bold claim He is "the resurrection and the life" (John 11:25) is so filled with hope.

When Jesus heard that His good friend Lazarus was ill, Jesus, the healer of the sick, did the unthinkable (in human terms) — He purposefully delayed two days before traveling to Lazarus' home (John 11:6). Jesus told His disciples that Lazarus' illness would not "*end* in death" (11:4, emphasis added), and He would prove that very claim.

When Jesus and His disciples arrived in Bethany, where Lazarus and his sisters Martha and Mary lived, Lazarus had indeed died — and had been in his tomb for four days (11:17). Martha,

In His own divine-

humanity, Jesus exhibits the

eternal life available to

mortal men and women who

are in union with Him.

through her tears, reaffirmed her faith in Jesus but wished

He had come quickly to heal her brother (11:21–22). Jesus assured her that Lazarus would rise again (11:23). And she, trusting in what the prophets taught (Isaiah 26:19; Daniel 12:2), proclaimed her belief in the doctrine of bodily resurrection at the end times, when the bodies of the dead will be reunited with their souls (John 11:24).

But what Martha declared as faith, Jesus declared as a fact. Jesus didn't tell her that He raises people from the dead — as if it were some parlor trick — though He did and would raise the dead (Luke 7:12–15; 8:49–55; John 11:43–44). He told Martha: "*I am* the resurrection and the life" (John 11:25, emphasis added). His purpose in raising Lazarus was to show that the hope of life in a world of death is rooted in the person *of* Jesus, not in a theological proposition *about* Jesus.

In His own divine-humanity, Jesus exhibits the eternal life available to mortal men and women who are in union with Him. Those who do not believe in Jesus exist in animated bodies but are dead, passing through a world of death to a destiny of eternal death in hell — forever separated from God. How utterly hopeless!

But for those who believe in Jesus, even if they die in their bodies, they will live in their spirits, to one day live in their bodies anew with Christ (John 11:25). This is what Jesus asked Martha to believe — that He is the victor over physical and spiritual death ("the resurrection"), and that He is the sustainer of a forever-kind of life ("the life").

Lazarus' illness carried with it the penalty of physical death, but it didn't *end* in death — even though he underwent physical death again. For no matter what happened to his body, Lazarus, at the point of belief, lives eternally in the presence of God. And a day will come for Lazarus and for all believers who have died in their bodies, when they will be rejoined forever with their bodies and souls made incorruptible — with Jesus in the new heaven and new earth (1 Thessalonians 4:14 – 16). This is the hope Jesus gave Martha and Mary and the hope we preach today (4:13, 18), because it is the only hope that can stare down death — it is the hope of resurrection and life.

— *Derrick G. Jeter*

THE WAY, THE TRUTH, THE LIFE

"I am the way,

and the truth,

and the life;

no one comes to

the Father but

through Me."

— John 14:6

We live in an age of tolerance, where everyone and everything is expected to be accepted . . . except those who make exclusive claims. Perhaps that's why so many reject Christ. He stands squarely in the street proclaiming: "I am the way, the truth, and the life" (John 14:6). No ifs, ands, or buts; no wiggle room; no hedging, halting, or haggling. The "tolerant" simply find this intolerable. Yet, our world is full of worn-down people who've tried every other way and come up empty. They don't need more options; they need the One and Only.

At least three times, Jesus told His disciples He must die and be raised from the dead (Mark 8:31–32; 9:30–32; 10:32–34). After His death and resurrection, Jesus told them the Father would glorify the Son and take Him to heaven (John 13:31–33). Peter, like the other disciples, didn't understand and wanted to know "where" Jesus was going (John 13:36). To the "Father's house," Jesus answered (14:1–3). But this didn't satisfy Thomas. Without knowing where the Father's house was, Thomas argued, how would they know the way (14:5)?

Thomas wanted an unambiguous answer. What he got was an enigmatic reply. The Lord comforted His disciples in the face of His impending death. But His death didn't mean they would never see Him again. They would go where He was going because they already knew the way . . . *because they already knew Him — the Way, the Truth, and the Life.*

The Way

Without a mediator an unholy humanity is eternally cut off from a holy God. But as the Way, Jesus reveals the right road to God, which presupposes there is a wrong road — the way of self. The way of Jesus leads to life, but the way of self leads to death (Romans 6:23). However,

ironically, the way to eternal life with Christ requires the death of self. And this is only accomplished by following the way of the cross — by accepting Christ's sacrificial death upon it and taking up our own (Matthew 16:24–25).

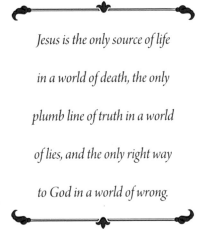

Jesus is the only source of life in a world of death, the only plumb line of truth in a world of lies, and the only right way to God in a world of wrong.

The Truth

Truth is that which perfectly corresponds to reality, and nothing is more real than God and His Word. As God, Jesus is truth because He embodies divine revelation as the trustworthy and salvific Word — the only teacher able to fully reveal God (John 1:1). Here again rests irony — for when Pilate stared Truth in the face and asked Jesus, "What is truth?" the official was so full of deceit, he couldn't recognize Truth staring back at him (John 18:38).

The Life

Life isn't about the here-and-now; life is about eternity. Life isn't just something; it's some-one. As the source, sustainer, and secret of life (John 11:25), in Jesus alone can we find abundant life on earth and eternal life in heaven (1 John 5:11–12). However, this again is ironic, because the life Jesus offers is only available because of the death He endured. But His death wasn't the end of the story. In the ultimate irony, after three days, death was defeated when the Life burst forth bodily from the tomb.

Jesus is the only source of life in a world of death, the only plumb line of truth in a world of lies, and the only right way to God in a world of wrong. Every other path leads to destruction. *The Way, the Truth, and the Life* — Jesus — is our only certain hope. May we commit ourselves to following Him and pointing others to Him, whether or not the world tolerates it.

— *Derrick G. Jeter*

LORD

"Therefore let all the house of Israel know for certain that God has made Him both Lord and Christ — this Jesus whom you crucified."

— Acts 2:36

Have you ever read a novel and couldn't wait to get to the end? You may have been so intrigued by the story that you just had to take a peek just to see what would happen. Turning to the last page might typically ruin a good story, but in the case of the Bible, it actually is a wonderful thing . . . because the ending gives us hope. Consider how the last passage sums up all sixty-six books: "The grace of the Lord Jesus be with all" (Revelation 22:21).

The word *lord* has rich meaning that spans the Bible. In the Old Testament, the term was used by the Israelites to describe God as owner or master. To be lord is to be the one to whom a person or thing belongs. The term carries the idea of a person who is sovereign over people and places and who is able to influence the course of history.

During most of Jesus' earthly ministry, the disciples' used the title *Lord* as more of a term of respect, as one designated to the lord of a household. But their view of Jesus changed with His death, burial, and resurrection. Those who believed then associated Jesus with the Lord of the Old Testament, the one to whom all authority was given. Peter announced on the day of Pentecost, "Therefore let all the house of Israel know for certain that God has made Him both Lord and Christ — this Jesus whom you crucified" (Acts 2:36). The resurrection changed everything!

Jesus' resurrection secured forgiveness of sins for all of us who trust in Him and in Jesus' unquestioned ownership over us as Lord (Romans 6:5; 1 Corinthians 6:20; 15:17). Because Jesus is the one worthy to receive praise and honor, believers must order our lives around the recognition of the lordship of Jesus . . . that we belong to Him and that we're willing to obey His will as conveyed through Scripture.

But what about His lordship over creation? When we observe all the chaos and upheaval in the world, we might wonder how it is that Jesus is Lord. If the title *Lord* means "to be in charge," it might seem at times that the Lord Jesus has taken a long lunch break. Sin and death have seeped into every crack and crevice of this world, with the expectation of getting worse before Jesus returns to put an end to sin and death, once for all.

No wonder John cried out at the end of Revelation for the Lord to come back and finish what He started. "Come, Lord Jesus" (Revelation 22:20). This phrase should resonate through our hearts because we know all is not right with the world. But we can be assured that God is indeed in control. Jesus will reign as Lord until all enemies have been abolished, including death. Then He will turn over His Kingdom to the Father, who will demonstrate His lordship over all (1 Corinthians 15:26–28). This

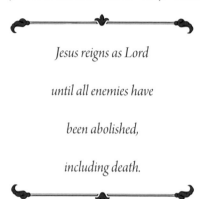

Jesus reigns as Lord

until all enemies have

been abolished,

including death.

is the very good news that comes at the end.

But how fascinating to see what follows this appeal for the Lord Jesus to return: a benediction for the grace of the Lord Jesus to be with us. This is God's last word to us, for the grace of our Lord to be with us. We need His grace to keep us going — to give us the endurance to live well within the chaos of our world. The Lord's grace sustains us and assures us of His sovereignty when we are tempted to fear and question His reign. We can be assured that He is in control. He is Lord who provides us grace and hope.

— *Lisa Robinson*

CORNERSTONE

You are … of

God's household, having

been built

on the foundation

of the apostles and

prophets, Christ Jesus

Himself being

the corner stone.

— Ephesians 2:19–20

hen one thinks of Jesus, *cornerstone* might not readily come to mind. A cornerstone holds two walls together and is the first stone laid that sets the bearings for a structure's walls. Builders use a cornerstone to support the entire foundation of a building. Without this anchor, a building can collapse because its walls would not be properly supported. It is fascinating to see how God uses this physical, architectural element to describe what He is doing spiritually through the life, death, and resurrection of Jesus.

The Old Testament set the stage. The cornerstone was used as a metaphor to describe the physical temple that God promised to David (1 Chronicles 17:10–14). The temple was the place where God's glory would dwell, where the people's sins would be forgiven. Jesus would ultimately fulfill this purpose. Psalm 118:22 tells us that the builders rejected what would be the cornerstone. While this referred to the physical temple, there is a connection to Jesus and

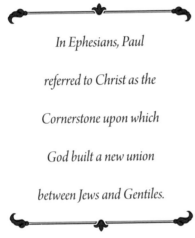

In Ephesians, Paul

referred to Christ as the

Cornerstone upon which

God built a new union

between Jews and Gentiles.

His church. Jesus, in quoting this psalm, let His listeners know that He is the Cornerstone whom the builders rejected (Luke 20:17). The builders — "the chief priests and the scribes with the elders" (20:1) — thought they were doing God's work, but in reality, they were holding on to their own, self-serving ways. Peter also identified this rejection in Acts 4:11. Jesus is the foundation on which all God's work stands.

In Ephesians, Paul referred to Christ as the Cornerstone upon which God built a new union between Jews and Gentiles — the church — united into one body, as fellow citizens of the household of God "built on the foundation of the apostles and prophets, Christ Jesus Himself being the corner stone" (Ephesians 2:20). In this context, the "building" consists of all those who believe in Christ. The holy temple is the church (2:21). That's us! The church is not a physical building — though the visible church certainly needs a physical infrastructure — but one built on the truth of the work and person of Jesus Christ. Christ is the measuring standard by which the church must conform.

What is the foundation of the apostles and prophets? The apostles testified to the risen Lord. They proclaimed that Jesus was the Son of God, the One appointed as the foundation for what God was building. Their divinely inspired words — Scripture — are to be believed regarding Jesus and His body. Christ and His church are inseparable. Therefore, what is true of Jesus is also true of His church.

Throughout history, the church has been challenged regarding its beliefs. To be sure, this opposition from both without and within has affected the church body. Some in the church — who claim to be doing God's work — have bowed to the opposition by either dismissing the church's foundational tenets or changing these tenets for acceptance and approval.

Just looking around today, it's plain to see that the cultural tide has turned against the church. As enticing as it might be to go with the flow to get along with today's culture, we must remember that without Christ as Anchor, the church can no longer be called a church, no matter how many good works it does or how good one of its preachers sounds. People will hate the church and ridicule it because these nonbelievers actually reject the Cornerstone.

But don't despair! Remember, the true church, the believers in union with Christ, have a sure foundation. Our Anchor, Christ, provides us hope because we who believe will not be put to shame (Isaiah 28:16; 1 Peter 2:6). Our beliefs might be unpopular and even ridiculed. But in the last days, our faithfulness toward Christ — the Cornerstone of the church — will be vindicated when He returns.

— *Lisa Robinson*

HEAD OF THE CHURCH

Christ also

is the head

of the church.

— Ephesians 5:23

The concept of someone being the head of something is prevalent in our society. Being the "head" of a company, organization, or government entity denotes leadership. No matter the realm, we consider the head as the one who wields authority and power — the person in charge and calling the shots.

Jesus, the Head of the church, certainly fits this bill. In Ephesians, Paul let us know that God the Father has handed all power and authority to God the Son: "He put all things in subjection under His feet, and gave Him as head over all things to the church" (Ephesians 1:22). "All things" means all creation. In other words, Jesus gets to dictate the terms of everything in the universe.

Paul did more than just give Jesus a title, though. The apostle went on to present a profound relationship for believers to consider — that between Jesus and the church. We might look at church as pro forma, just something we should do as Christians. But that falls flat! The church is more than the group of people we meet with on Sundays. The church is *all* who are united in Christ; it's the *body* of Christ. The church consists of those who have been invited to participate in God's divine program, through belief in its Head, Jesus Christ. It's a positional relationship that describes our identity as believers.

It's also a dynamic relationship of submission to the Head because of His sacrificial love for us. Just look at how Paul described the marriage relationship as a metaphor for Christ's love for His church (Ephesians 5:22 – 33)! It's tough to tell when Paul stopped talking about marriage and started talking about the church.

So, Jesus as Head of the church means more than just His holding a position of authority and power, although He does. This name of Jesus has implications for *our* growth because of the interdependent relationship between the Head and the body. His headship fuels the life of believers, and we are to grow up *in* Him, meaning that how we live, what we think, and what we believe must be anchored in Christ. That's refreshingly good news for us! It lets us off the hook for coming up with ways to "measure up." He's already told us how through His word and His example.

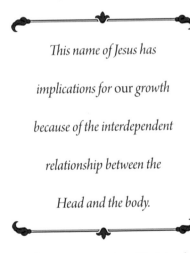

This name of Jesus has implications for our growth because of the interdependent relationship between the Head and the body.

Growing up in Christ also means that our relationships with one another must be anchored in Christ. We grow up in Christ as we speak the truth in love to one another (Ephesians 4:15). What truth? The truth of Jesus — who He is and what that means for us. Speaking the truth in love means confronting behavior and beliefs that contradict the truth of Jesus. When we speak the truth of the Head, it fuels the church body to grow in Him.

We are not automatons that obey the Head because He says so; rather, Christ's authority in our lives translates into our love for Him and for each other. Here is where the dynamic relationship between the Head and His body takes on even more significance. People outside the church don't see the Head, but they do see His body. Is it any wonder why Paul proclaimed the sweeping majesty of Christ in the same breath as His headship over the church? The church should be a living portrait of its Head!

That ought to compel us to think about how we honor Jesus as Head. Do we submit to His authority? Do we honor His church by reflecting the sacrificial love He showed us? What image of Christ are we exhibiting for the world to see?

— *Lisa Robinson*

MEDIATOR

For there is

one God, and one

mediator also between

God and men,

the man Christ Jesus.

— 1 Timothy 2:5

Some of the people most important to the functioning of a civil society are also some of the most overlooked. Without them, however, games would descend into bloodbaths, legal disputes would become ever-revolving cycles of claims and counterclaims, and troubled marriages would all end in divorce. To keep these things from happening, we need referees, judges, and counselors — mediators.

Although as old as humanity, the first mediator wasn't human; He was divine. When Adam and Eve disobeyed God's command to abstain from eating the fruit from the Tree of the Knowledge of Good and Evil (Genesis 2:17; 3:6), God mediated between His justice and His mercy, sacrificing an animal to make clothes for the couple to cover their blame and shame (3:21).

But not until Job, in the midst of his suffering, accused by his three friends of sinning, did the idea of a divine mediator come into sharper focus. Job complained that God wasn't a man whom he could take to court (Job 9:32), and he lamented that there was no one to serve as an "umpire" between God and His suffering servant — no one who could understand the justice of God and the frailty of humanity and "who may lay his hand upon us both" (9:33).

In time, God did provide someone who could fulfill Job's longing, one who could wear the robe of divinity and the flesh of humanity simultaneously — Jesus Christ (Hebrews 4:14 – 15).

God's great desire is that all people would come to saving faith (2 Peter 3:9) although He knows not all will. Without Christ, none of us can know the joy of salvation. Without Christ, all of us, spiritually speaking, are enemies of God, separated from Him and opposed to Him because of our sin (Romans 5:10). That's what makes the doctrine of mediation so magnificent. Jesus is our source of reconciliation and friendship with God!

In 1 Timothy 2:5, Paul described God in Old Testament terms — He is "one." This truth is found in the first command of the Decalogue (Exodus 20:2 – 5) and the great *shema* of Israel: "Hear, O Israel! The LORD is our God, the LORD is one!" (Deuteronomy 6:4). The oneness of God, or as the New Living Translation renders it, "The LORD is our God, the LORD alone," highlights the exclusive aspect of salvation. No other God exists. So salvation is found in no other — only in God alone.

However, the one God (*eis Theos*) is juxtaposed to the "one mediator" (*eis mesites*) — the go-between betwixt a holy God and an unholy humanity. Access to salvation is universal — all *can* come to saving faith — but the application of salvation is particular. Only through the mediator, the divine person of Jesus Christ, can sinful people be at peace with a sinless God (1 Timothy 2:5).

Christ is the only mediator between God and humankind, because He is the only one who

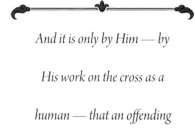

And it is only by Him — by

His work on the cross as a

human — that an offending

humanity can be reconciled to

an offended God.

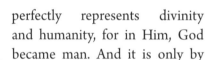

perfectly represents divinity and humanity, for in Him, God became man. And it is only by

Him — by His work on the cross as a human — that an offending humanity can be reconciled to an offended God (2:6).

The foundation of our faith is that Jesus, the mediator between holy God and unholy humanity, gave His life on the cross as a willing sacrifice to atone for our sins and to offer us peace with God. Pleased with Jesus' sacrifice, God raised Him from the dead and promised that all who believe will inherit the treasures of the new covenant. To know Jesus by the name Mediator is to know God by the name Father and to have life eternal and redemption forever (Hebrews 8:6; 9:15; 12:24).

— Derrick G. Jeter

HIGH PRIEST

Therefore, He

had to be made like

His brethren in all things,

so that He might

become a merciful

and faithful high priest

in things pertaining

to God, to make

propitiation for the

sins of the people.

— Hebrews 2:17

What do most people know about priests or the priesthood? Chances are not very much, especially if they're Protestant Christians. And if they do know something *intellectually* about priests — say, in the case of Catholic priests, that they're men dedicated to lifelong, celibate service to God — most people know next to nothing *experientially* about priests. Not even most Jews — whose religious history and tradition has been rich in the priesthood since the destruction of the Jerusalem temple in AD 70 — have firsthand experience with priests.

Yet, when we come to the book of Hebrews, the most distinctive illustration we find is the image of Jesus as our High Priest. The writer to the Hebrews painted a portrait of Christ as superior to Old Testament Levitical priests because His gospel — the complete, final, once-for-all sacrifice of His body and blood — is superior to the old sacrificial system. Unlike priests of old, Jesus didn't pass through a tabernacle made with human hands or offer to God the sacrifice of animals; rather He passed through the heavenly tabernacle and offered the sacrifice of Himself (Hebrews 9:11).

That's why Jesus, as our High Priest, became a man—so He might show us mercy and prove faithful to God the Father, in order to "make propitiation [atonement] for the sins of the people" (2:17). Because of this, we are exhorted to ponder the truth that Jesus is both God's messenger to humanity and our High Priest, serving as believers' representative to God (3:1). In this way, Jesus, like Moses, was faithful to His calling. But unlike Moses, Jesus was superior in His faithfulness to God (3:2–3).

Inspired by Jesus' faithfulness, we, too, should remain faithful to our confession of faith, deriving courage from the fact that our High Priest suffered temptation as we do but without succumbing (4:14–15). Because of His firsthand experience of battling and winning over temptation, Jesus understands our struggle and is able to show us mercy.

And through His mercy and faithfulness, Christ passed through the veil separating God and humanity and became for those who believe in Him a priest in the order of Melchizedek (5:10; 6:20), which literally means "righteous king." Melchizedek was probably a title rather than a proper name, and the man who bore the title served as a prototype of Christ in that he was both a king and a priest (7:1) whose rule and role was characterized by righteousness and peace (Psalm 85:10; Isaiah 32:17; Hebrews 7:2).

Jesus is not only superior to any other priest; He is superior to any other person (7:26). He alone is holy (blameless of sin), innocent (without guile or malice), undefiled (absolutely pure), and separate from sinners (above and beyond all creation). Jesus is placed in a different

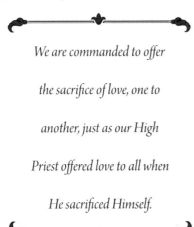

We are commanded to offer

the sacrifice of love, one to

another, just as our High

Priest offered love to all when

He sacrificed Himself.

category from sinful people as the only One who was born holy, who remained holy while on earth, and who continues to be holy with authority and power, seated at the right hand of God in heaven where He ministers to the saints forever (Hebrews 8:1–2).

Technically, because He comes from the tribe of Judah, not Levi, Jesus isn't allowed to serve as our High Priest — according to Levitical Law. And yet, He serves. For this reason, the Law was changed (7:12), and now we who worship under the ministry of Jesus are not under Levitical Law; we are under a new and better law — the law of love (John 13:34–35). As such, we are commanded to offer the sacrifice of love, one to another, just as our High Priest offered love to all when He sacrificed Himself (1 John 3:11).

— *Derrick G. Jeter*

SAVIOR

We have seen

and testify that

the Father has sent

the Son to be the

Savior of the world.

— 1 John 4:14

he Christian faith only makes sense within the context of salvation. As weak and needy humans, we've always required divine deliverance from sin without and from sin within — sin from others, sin from the natural world, and sin from ourselves. And sprinkled throughout Scripture are dozens of references to the Lord Himself as Rescuer or as Savior.

Savior comes from the word *save* — *yasha* in Hebrew and *sozo* in Greek. In the Old Testament contexts, the word was most often used in reference to physical deliverance, as from a trial or danger. King David, "in the day that the LORD delivered him" (2 Samuel 22:1) from King Saul's deadly machinations, began his song of thanksgiving like this:

"The LORD is my rock
and my fortress and
my deliverer;
My God, my rock, in
whom I take refuge,
My shield and the horn
of my salvation, my
stronghold and my
refuge;
My savior, You save
me from violence."
(2 Samuel 22:2–3;
expanded in
Psalm 18)

In Isaiah 43:11, Yahweh declared, "I, even I, am the LORD, and there is no savior besides Me." We should remember this as we jump to the New Testament and meet Mary the mother of Jesus. Newly pregnant, carrying the long-awaited Messiah, Mary visited her cousin Elizabeth and showed that she knew her theology. As they greeted one another, Mary sang, "My soul exalts the Lord, / And my spirit has rejoiced in God my Savior" (Luke 1:46–47).

Just a few paragraphs later in the same gospel, an angel announced Jesus' birth to the shepherds. Christmas pageant veterans and *A Charlie Brown Christmas* fans alike will recognize this defining phrase: "For today in the city of David there has been born for you a Savior, who is Christ the Lord" (2:11).

"Born for you a Savior" . . . it was for this reason that Jesus came. His overwhelming purpose was to bring glory to God the Father by saving His people. But unlike the Old Testament, the New Testament writers emphasized *Savior* in reference to our need for spiritual salvation from sin's power and consequences. By His living, dying, and rising again, Jesus offers forgiveness to all who would accept His substitutionary sacrifice. Only by that forgiveness are we saved from sure death — eternal separation from God — into everlasting life.

Referring to Jesus, the apostle Peter defied the Jewish religious leaders with these words, "He is the one whom God exalted to His right hand as a Prince and a Savior, to grant repentance to Israel, and forgiveness of sins" (Acts 5:31). And Paul often referred to Jesus as Savior, using the title to explain the spiritual repercussions of our salvation: "Our Savior Christ Jesus, who abolished death and brought life and immortality to light through the gospel" (2 Timothy 1:10).

This salvation, we see, is based solely on Jesus' actions on our behalf. It is a gift from our Savior: "But when the kindness of God our Savior and His love for mankind appeared, He saved us, not on the basis of deeds which we have done in righteousness, but according to His mercy" (Titus 3:4–5).

At the cross, our Savior paid the price for our sin. He offered Himself in our place, satisfying God's wrath toward sin and sinners. Those who try to save

He offered Himself

in our place, satisfying

God's wrath toward

sin and sinners.

themselves will fall woefully short. So may we be as the apostle John, who said, "We have seen and testify that the Father has sent the Son to be the Savior of the world" (1 John 4:14).

— *Kelley Mathews*

ALPHA AND OMEGA

I n the opening lines of the book of Revelation, God used a cultural metaphor to describe Himself: " 'I am the Alpha and the Omega,' says the Lord God, 'who is and who was and who is to come, the Almighty' " (Revelation 1:8). Such language would have sounded familiar in the ears of the apostle John and his Greek-speaking readers. *Alpha* is the first letter of the Greek alphabet; *Omega* is the last.

Through John's pen, God repeated this name, with a twist, in Revelation 21:6: "Then He [God] said to me, 'It is done. I am the Alpha and the Omega, the beginning and the end.' " Whenever something is repeated in the Bible, the purpose is emphasis. So our ears should perk up here, as well as later in Revelation 22:13 when Jesus claimed the title as well: "I am the Alpha and the Omega, the first and the last, the beginning and the end."

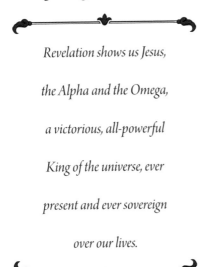

Revelation shows us Jesus,

the Alpha and the Omega,

a victorious, all-powerful

King of the universe, ever

present and ever sovereign

over our lives.

"The first and the last, the beginning and the end" — these extrapolations reflect God's eternal being and His timelessness. It's a name that says, "I was there in the beginning, I've been here all along, and I will be here at the end." Jewish believers reading John's book would have heard echoes of "I Am" (Yahweh), God's personal name for Himself that points to His eternality. (See Exodus 3:14; Isaiah 41:4; 43:10; 44:6.)

For Jesus to also declare that He is the Alpha and Omega reveals His equality with God Almighty.[1] Jesus, the second person of the Trinity, was also present at creation. We read in John 1:1–2, "In the beginning was the Word, and the Word was with God, and the Word was God. He was in the beginning with God." In John's gospel, Jesus also laid claim to "I Am" (John 8:58), directly asserting His deity. Before He was born as a man in first-century Israel, Jesus existed outside of time along with His Father and the Holy Spirit. He was present at the beginning of time, and He will be present at the end of time.

"Alpha and Omega" implies more than just eternal existence. It also asserts preeminence, authority, and sovereignty. When an English speaker claims to know something "from A to Z," that person is claiming a comprehensive, exhaustive, masterful knowledge. In a similar way, "Alpha and Omega" indicates the complete power and faithful sovereignty of God and His Son, Jesus, over creation. This wouldn't have been lost on John's original readers. "The combination of alpha and omega in secular literature came to designate the entire universe and all kinds of divine and demonic powers, so that in Revelation this title could refer to Christ's dominion over the universe."[2]

We serve a living and powerful God who created the earth, set in motion a plan to redeem the earth, and will one day judge the earth and all its people. Revelation shows us Jesus — the Alpha and the Omega; the victorious, all-powerful King of the universe; the ever present and ever sovereign Lord over our lives. We are invited to fear Him as judge or worship Him as King. Come, let us worship and bow down.

— *Kelley Mathews*

1. A. T. Robertson, *Word Pictures in the New Testament: The General Epistles, the Revelation of John*, vol. 6 (Nashville: Broadman Press, 1933), Revelation 22:13.
2. Johannes P. Louw and Eugene Albert Nida, *Greek-English Lexicon of the New Testament: Based on Semantic Domains*, 2nd ed. (New York: United Bible Societies, 1996), 611.

APPENDIX

NAMES OF JESUS WITH BIBLE REFERENCES

NAME	BIBLE REFERENCE
Advocate	1 John 2:1
Alpha and Omega	Revelation 1:8; 21:6; 22:13
The Amen	Revelation 3:14
Ancient of Days	Daniel 7:22
Angel of the LORD	Genesis 16:7, 9, 10, 11; 22:11, 15
	Exodus 3:2
	Numbers 22:22–27, 31, 32, 34, 35
	Judges 2:1, 4; 5:23; 6:11, 12, 21, 22; 13:3, 15, 16, 17, 18, 20, 21
	2 Samuel 24:16
	1 Kings 19:7
	2 Kings 1:3, 15; 19:35
	1 Chronicles 21:12, 15, 16, 18, 30
	Psalm 34:7; 35:5, 6
	Isaiah 37:36
	Zechariah 1:11, 12; 3:1, 5, 6; 12:8
Author and Perfecter of Our Faith	Hebrews 12:2

NAME	BIBLE REFERENCE
Beginning	Colossians 1:18
Beloved/Beloved Son	Matthew 3:17; 12:18; 17:5
	Mark 1:11; 9:7
	Luke 3:22
	2 Peter 1:17
Branch	Isaiah 4:2; 11:1
	Jeremiah 23:5; 33:15
	Zechariah 3:8; 6:12
Bread of God	John 6:33
Bread of Life	John 6:35; 6:48
Bridegroom	Matthew 9:15; 25:1, 5, 6, 10
	Mark 2:19, 20
	Luke 5:34, 35
	Revelation 18:23
Bright Morning Star	Revelation 22:16
Carpenter	Mark 6:3
Chief Shepherd	1 Peter 5:4
Christ	Matthew 16:16, plus more than 500 other occurrences in the New Testament
Cornerstone	Matthew 21:42
	Mark 12:10
	Luke 20:17
	Acts 4:11
	Ephesians 2:20
	1 Peter 2:6, 7
Deliverer	Romans 11:26
Door	John 10:7, 9
Eternal Father	Isaiah 9:6
Everlasting Father	Isaiah 9:6

NAME	BIBLE REFERENCE
Faithful Witness	Revelation 1:5
Faithful and True Witness	Revelation 3:14
Firstborn of All Creation	Colossians 1:15
Firstborn of / from the Dead	Colossians 1:18
	Revelation 1:5
Good Shepherd	John 10:11, 14
Great Shepherd	Hebrews 13:20
Guardian of Souls	1 Peter 2:25
Head of the Body	Colossians 1:18
Head of the Church	Ephesians 1:22; 4:15; 5:23
	Colossians 1:18
High Priest	Hebrews 2:17; 3:1; 4:14, 15; 5:10; 6:20; 7:26; 8:1; 9:11
Holy One	Psalm 16:10
	Mark 1:24
	Luke 4:34
	John 6:69
	Acts 2:27; 3:14; 13:15
	1 Peter 1:15
	1 John 2:20
	Revelation 16:5
Horn of Salvation	Luke 1:69
I Am	Exodus 3:14
	Mark 14:62
	John 8:58
Image of God	2 Corinthians 4:4
	Colossians 1:15
Immanuel	Isaiah 7:14; 8:8
	Matthew 1:23

NAME	BIBLE REFERENCE
Jesus	Name appears more than 900 times in the New Testament
Judge	Acts 10:42
	2 Timothy 4:8
	James 4:12; 5:9
King	Matthew 21:5; 25:34, 40; 27:42
	Luke 19:38; 23:2
	John 1:49; 12:13, 15; 18:37; 19:14, 15
	Acts 17:7
	1 Timothy 6:15
King of the Jews	Matthew 2:2; 27:11, 29, 37
	Mark 15:2, 9, 12, 18, 26, 32
	Luke 23:3, 37, 38
	John 18:33, 39; 19:3, 19, 21
King of Kings	1 Timothy 6:15
	Revelation 17:14; 19:16
Lamb / Lamb of God	John 1:29, 36
	Revelation 5:6; 6:9; 7:17; 14:10; 15:3; 17:14; 19:9; 21:23; 22:1, 3
Last Adam	1 Corinthians 15:45
Light of the World	John 8:12; 9:5
Lion of the Tribe of Judah	Revelation 5:5
Living Stone	1 Peter 2:4
Lord	Name appears numerous times in the New Testament, including Revelation 22:21
Lord of Lords	1 Timothy 6:15
	Revelation 17:14; 19:16
Lord of All	Acts 10:36
	Romans 10:12

NAME	BIBLE REFERENCE
Man of Sorrows	Isaiah 53:3
Master	Luke 5:5; 8:24, 45; 9:33, 49; 17:13
	Ephesians 6:9
	Colossians 4:1
	2 Timothy 2:21
	2 Peter 2:1
	Jude 1:4
Mediator	1 Timothy 2:5
	Hebrews 8:6; 9:15; 12:24
Messiah	Daniel 9:25, 26
	Matthew 1:1, 16, 17; 2:4
	John 1:41; 4:25
Messiah the Prince	Daniel 9:25
Mighty God	Isaiah 9:6
Only Begotten Son	John 3:16, 18
	1 John 4:9
Overseer of Souls	1 Peter 2:25
Prince	Acts 5:31
Prince of Peace	Isaiah 9:6
Prince of Life	Acts 3:15
Prophet	Matthew 21:11, 46
	John 6:14; 7:40; 9:17
Rabbi/Rabboni	Matthew 26:25, 49
	Mark 9:5; 10:51; 11:21; 14:45
	John 1:38, 49; 3:2; 4:31; 6:25; 9:2; 11:8; 20:16
Resurrection and Life	John 11:25
Righteous One	Acts 3:14; 7:52; 22:14
Rock	1 Corinthians 10:4

Name	Bible Reference
Root/Root of David/Root of Jesse	Romans 15:12
	Revelation 5:5; 22:16
Savior	Luke 2:11
	John 4:42
	Acts 5:31; 13:23
	Ephesians 5:23
	Philippians 3:20
	2 Timothy 1:10
	Titus 1:4; 2:13; 3:6
	2 Peter 1:1, 11; 2:20; 3:2, 18
	1 John 4:14
Second Man	1 Corinthians 15:47
Servant	Matthew 12:18
	Acts 3:13, 26; 4:27, 30
	Romans 15:8
Shepherd	John 10:11, 14
	1 Peter 2:25
Shepherd and Bishop	1 Peter 2:25 (KJV)
Shepherd, Chief	See "Chief Shepherd"
Shepherd, Good	See "Good Shepherd"
Shiloh	Genesis 49:10
Son of David	Matthew 1:1; 9:27; 12:23; 15:22; 20:30, 31; 21:9, 15; 22:42;
	Mark 10:47, 48; 12:35
	Luke 18:38, 39

NAME	BIBLE REFERENCE
Son of God	Matthew 4:3, 6; 8:29; 26:63; 27:40, 43, 54
	Mark 1:1; 3:11; 15:39
	Luke 1:35; 4:3, 9, 41; 22:70
	John 1:34, 49; 3:18; 5:25; 10:36; 11:4, 27; 19:7; 20:31
	Acts 8:37; 9:20
	Romans 1:4
	2 Corinthians 1:19
	Galatians 2:20
	Ephesians 4:13
	Hebrews 4:14; 6:6; 7:3; 10:29
	1 John 3:8; 4:15; 5:5, 10, 12, 13, 20
	Revelation 2:18
Son of Man	Matthew 8:20; 9:6; 10:23; 11:19; 12:8, 32, 40; 13:37, 41; 16:13, 27, 28; 17:9, 12, 22; 18:11; 19:28; 20:18, 28; 24:27, 30, 37, 39, 44; 25:31; 26:2, 24, 45, 64
	Mark 2:10; et al
	Luke 5:24; et al
	John 1:51; et al
	Acts 7:56
	Hebrews 2:6
	Revelation 1:13; 14:14
Son of the Father	2 John 1:3
Son of the Living God	Matthew 16:16
Son of the Most High / Son of the Most High God	Mark 5:7
	Luke 1:32; 8:28

NAME	BIBLE REFERENCE
Sun of Righteousness	Malachi 4:2
True God	1 John 5:20
True Vine	John 15:1
Vine	John 15:5
Way, Truth, Life	John 14:6
Witness	Revelation 3:14
Wonderful Counselor	Isaiah 9:6
Word	John 1:1, 14
	1 John 1:1
	Revelation 19:12–13

HOW TO BEGIN A RELATIONSHIP WITH GOD

In the light of Jesus' perfect holiness, our righteousness withers away. We are broken, flawed, and in terrible need of wholeness and reconciliation with God. Thankfully, we are not left alone in our wretched state, because God has made a way back to Him—not based on our efforts, which will fail, or our fortunes, which will fade, but through His Son, Jesus, whose sacrificial death on our behalf pardons us from sin and frees us to live peaceably with God, forever. From Genesis to Revelation, God reveals four essential truths we all must accept and apply if we are to find the life-transforming remedy for our sin-sick souls. Let's look at these four truths in detail.

Our Spiritual Condition: Totally Depraved

The first truth is rather personal. One look in the mirror of Scripture, and our human condition becomes painfully clear:

"There is none righteous, not even one;
There is none who understands,
There is none who seeks for God;
All have turned aside, together they have become useless;
There is none who does good,
There is not even one." (Romans 3:10 – 12)

We are all sinners through and through — totally depraved. Now, that doesn't mean we've committed every atrocity known to humankind. We're not as *bad* as we can be, just as *bad off* as we can be. Sin colors all our thoughts, motives, words, and actions.

If you've been around a while, you likely already believe it. Look around. Everything around us bears the smudge marks of our sinful nature. Despite our best efforts to create a perfect world, crime statistics continue to soar, divorce rates keep climbing, and families keep crumbling.

Something has gone terribly wrong in our society and in ourselves — something deadly. Contrary to how the world would repackage it, "me-first" living doesn't equal rugged individuality and freedom; it equals death. As Paul said in his letter to the Romans, "The wages of sin is death" (6:23) — our spiritual and physical death that comes from God's righteous judgment of our sin, along with all of the emotional and practical effects of this separation that we experience on a daily basis. This brings us to the second marker: God's character.

CHAPTER:VERSE

God's Character: Infinitely Holy

How can God judge us for a sinful state we were born into? Our total depravity is only half the answer. The other half is God's infinite holiness.

The fact that we know things are not as they should be points us to a standard of goodness beyond ourselves. Our sense of injustice in life on this side of eternity implies a perfect standard of justice beyond our reality. That standard and source is God Himself. And God's standard of holiness contrasts starkly with our sinful condition.

Scripture says that "God is Light, and in Him there is no darkness at all" (1 John 1:5). God is absolutely holy — which creates a problem for us. If He is so pure, how can we who are so impure relate to Him?

Perhaps we could try being better people, try to tilt the balance in favor of our good deeds, or seek out methods for self-improvement. Throughout history, people have attempted to live up to God's standard by keeping the Ten Commandments or living by their own code of ethics. Unfortunately, no one can come close to satisfying the demands of God's law. Romans 3:20 says, "By the works of the Law no flesh will be justified in His sight; for through the Law comes the knowledge of sin."

Our Need: A Substitute

So here we are, sinners by nature and sinners by choice, trying to pull ourselves up by our own bootstraps to attain a relationship with our holy Creator. But every time we try, we fall flat on our faces. We can't live a good enough life to make up for our sin, because God's standard isn't "good enough" — it's *perfection*. And we can't make amends for the offense our sin has created without dying for it.

Who can get us out of this mess?

If someone could live perfectly, honoring God's law, and would bear sin's death penalty for us — in our place — then we would be saved from our predicament. But is there such a person? Thankfully, yes!

Meet your substitute — *Jesus Christ.* He is the One who took death's place for you!

> [God] made [Jesus Christ] who knew no sin to be sin on our behalf, so that we might become the righteousness of God in Him. (2 Corinthians 5:21)

God's Provision: A Savior

God rescued us by sending His Son, Jesus, to die on the cross for our sins (1 John 4:9 – 10). Jesus was fully human and fully divine (John 1:1, 18), a truth that ensures His understanding of our weaknesses, His power to forgive, and His ability to bridge the gap between God and us (Romans 5:6 – 11). In short, we are "justified as a gift by His grace through the redemption which is in Christ Jesus" (Romans 3:24). Two words in this verse bear further explanation: *justified* and *redemption.*

Justification is God's act of mercy, in which He declares righteous the believing sinners while we are still in our sinning state. Justification doesn't mean that God *makes* us righteous, so that we never sin again, rather that He *declares* us righteous — much like a judge pardons a guilty criminal. Because Jesus took our sin upon Himself and suffered our judgment on the cross, God forgives our debt and proclaims us PARDONED.

Redemption is Christ's act of paying the complete price to release us from sin's bondage. God sent His Son to bear His wrath for all of our sins — past, present, and future (Romans 3:24 – 26; 2 Corinthians 5:21). In humble obedience, Christ willingly endured the shame of the cross for our sake (Mark 10:45; Romans 5:6 – 8; Philippians 2:8). Christ's death satisfied God's righteous demands. He no longer holds our sins against us, because His own Son paid the penalty for them. We are freed from the slave market of sin, never to be enslaved again!

Placing Your Faith in Christ

These four truths describe how God has provided a way to Himself through Jesus Christ. Because the price has been paid in full by God, we must respond to His free gift of eternal life in total faith and confidence in Him to save us. We must step forward into the relationship with God that He has prepared for us — not by doing good works or by being a good person, but by coming to Him just as we are and accepting His justification and redemption by faith.

> For by grace you have been saved through faith; and that not of yourselves, it is the gift of God; not as a result of works, so that no one may boast. (Ephesians 2:8 – 9)

We accept God's gift of salvation simply by placing our faith in Christ alone for the forgiveness of our sins. Would you like to enter a relationship with your Creator by trusting in Christ as your Savior? If so, here's a simple prayer you can use to express your faith:

> *Dear God,*
>
> *I know that my sin has put a barrier between You and me. Thank You for sending Your Son, Jesus, to die in my place. I trust in Jesus alone to forgive my sins, and I accept His gift of eternal life. I ask Jesus to be my personal Savior and the Lord of my life. Thank You. In Jesus' name, amen.*

If you've prayed this prayer or one like it and you wish to find out more about knowing God and His plan for you in the Bible, contact us at Insight for Living Ministries. Our contact information is provided on the following pages.

CHAPTER:VERSE

WE ARE HERE FOR YOU

If you desire to find out more about knowing God and His plan for you in the Bible, contact us. Insight for Living Ministries provides staff pastors who are available for free written correspondence or phone consultation. These seminary-trained and seasoned counselors have years of experience and are well-qualified guides for your spiritual journey.

Please feel welcome to contact your regional office by using the information below.

United States
Insight for Living Ministries
Biblical Counseling Department
Post Office Box 5000
Frisco, Texas 75034-0055
USA
972-473-5097 (Monday through Friday, 8:00 a.m. – 5:00 p.m. central time)
www.insight.org / contactapastor

Canada

Insight for Living Canada
Biblical Counseling Department
PO Box 8 Stn A
Abbotsford BC V2T 6Z4
CANADA
1-800-663-7639
info@insightforliving.ca

Australia, New Zealand, and South Pacific

Insight for Living Australia
Pastoral Care
Post Office Box 443
Boronia, VIC 3155
AUSTRALIA
+61 3 9762 6613

United Kingdom and Europe

Insight for Living United
  Kingdom
Pastoral Care
PO Box 553
Dorking
RH4 9EU
UNITED KINGDOM
0800 787 9364
+44 1306 640156
pastoralcare@insightforliving.org.uk

RESOURCES FOR PROBING FURTHER

How inspiring it is to read about the names of Jesus! His incredible ministry, His fulfillment of prophecy, His right to rule, His flawless life and service are of inexhaustible value. It's natural to want to continue examining the significance behind the names of Jesus Christ. Delving into further study is an exciting endeavor — there are literally volumes of books to supplement your study. We have compiled a list of books to assist you in discovering more.

Keep in mind as you read these books that we can't always endorse everything a writer or ministry says, so we encourage you to approach these and all resources with wisdom and discernment.

Bock, Darrell L. *Who Is Jesus: Linking the Historical Jesus with the Christ of Faith.* New York: Howard Books, 2012.

Insight for Living. *Insight's Bible Handbook: Practical Helps for Bible Study.* Plano, Tex.: IFL Publishing House, 2007.

Morgan, G. Campbell. *Life Applications from Every Chapter in the Bible.* Grand Rapids: Fleming H. Revell, 1994.

Packer, James I., Merrill C. Tenney, and William White, Jr., eds. *Illustrated Manners and Customs of the Bible.* Nashville: Thomas Nelson, 1980.

Swindoll, Charles R. *David: A Man of Passion & Destiny.* Great Lives Series. Nashville: Thomas Nelson, 2008.

Swindoll, Charles R. *Jesus: The Greatest Life of All.* Great Lives Series. Nashville: Thomas Nelson, 2008.

Swindoll, Charles R. *Swindoll's New Testament Insights: Insights on 1 & 2 Peter.* Grand Rapids: Zondervan, 2010.

Swindoll, Charles R. *Swindoll's New Testament Insights: Insights on John.* Grand Rapids: Zondervan, 2010.

Swindoll, Charles R. *Swindoll's New Testament Insights: Insights on Revelation.* Grand Rapids: Zondervan, 2011.

Walvoord, John F. and Roy B. Zuck, eds. *The Bible Knowledge Commentary: An Exposition of the Scriptures by Dallas Seminary Faculty, Old Testament.* Wheaton, Ill.: Victor Books, 1986.

Yancey, Philip. *The Jesus I Never Knew.* Grand Rapids: Zondervan, 1995.

ABOUT THE WRITERS

Derrick G. Jeter
Th.M., Dallas Theological Seminary

Derrick served as a writer for the Creative Ministries Department of Insight for Living Ministries. He has authored or coauthored more than twenty-five books. Derrick's writing has appeared on influential Web sites, and he is a contributing writer for *The Christian Post*. He and his wife, Christy, have five children and live in the Dallas area. He blogs at www.DerrickJeter.com.

Kelley Mathews
Th.M., Dallas Theological Seminary

Kelley serves as editor-in-chief for Authenticity Book House, a nonprofit Christian publisher. Kelley coauthored five books and freelanced as a writer and copy editor for more than fifteen years. An avid fiction reader, she is also a *Publishers Weekly* reviewer. Kelley and her husband, John, live with their four young children in the North Texas area.

Lisa Robinson
Th.M., Dallas Theological Seminary

Lisa has a passion for helping others think with a Christian worldview about God and life, and she blogs frequently at www.theothoughts.com. She also aspires to write popular-level theology books that connect with life experience. Lisa has been a nonprofit professional for more than twenty years. Widowed in 2004, Lisa lives in Dallas with her son.

Sharifa Stevens
Th.M., Dallas Theological Seminary

A New York native, Sharifa earned a bachelor of arts degree from Columbia University before moving to Dallas, Texas, to pursue a master's degree. She currently serves as a writer for the Creative Ministries Department of Insight for Living Ministries. Sharifa is passionate about worship through music and the intersection of faith and culture. She is wife to a Renaissance man and mother to two lively boys.

ORDERING INFORMATION

If you would like to order additional copies of *Names of Jesus* or other Insight for Living Ministries resources, please contact the office that serves you.

United States

Insight for Living Ministries
Post Office Box 5000
Frisco, Texas 75034-0055
USA
1-800-772-8888
(Monday through Friday,
    7:00 a.m. – 7:00 p.m. central time)
www.insight.org
www.insightworld.org

Canada

Insight for Living Canada
PO Box 8 Stn A
Abbotsford BC V2T 6Z4
CANADA
1-800-663-7639
www.insightforliving.ca

Australia, New Zealand, and South Pacific

Insight for Living Australia
Post Office Box 443
Boronia, VIC 3155
AUSTRALIA
+61 3 9762 6613
www.insight.asn.au

United Kingdom and Europe

Insight for Living United
  Kingdom
PO Box 553
Dorking
RH4 9EU
UNITED KINGDOM
0800 787 9364
+44 1306 640156
www.insightforliving.org.uk

Other International Locations

International constituents
may contact the U.S. office
through our Web site
(www.insightworld.org),
mail queries, or by calling
+1-972-473-5136.